The A to Z of Cooking

The A *to* Z *of Cooking*

Cathay Books

Scampi, apple and cheese salad

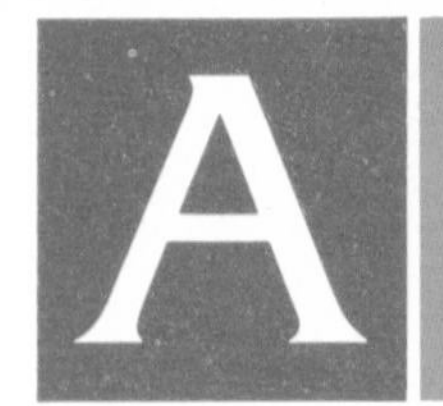

A *is for . . .* ADVENTUROUS APPETIZERS: *start a dinner party or special family supper with a new and exciting idea . . .* AFTER-SCHOOL SNACKS: *welcome home your hungry young scholars with something nourishing to tide them over until suppertime*

Adventurous Appetizers

SCAMPI, APPLE AND CHEESE SALAD

IMPERIAL/METRIC	AMERICAN
8 oz. (200 grms.) ricotta or cottage cheese	*8 oz. ricotta or cottage cheese*
3 oz. (75 grms.) chopped toasted nuts	*$\frac{1}{2}$ cup chopped toasted nuts*
escarole, Batavian endive or lettuce	*escarole, curly endive or lettuce*
1 dessert apple, cored, sliced and brushed with lemon juice	*1 dessert apple, cored, sliced and brushed with lemon juice*
12 to 16 fresh or frozen scampi or large shrimps, shelled	*12 to 16 fresh or frozen scampi or prawns, shelled*
Dressing	Dressing
3 tablespoons oil	*3 tablespoons oil*
1 tablespoon lemon juice	*1 tablespoon lemon juice*
salt and pepper	*salt and pepper*
$\frac{1}{2}$ avocado pear, mashed	*$\frac{1}{2}$ avocado pear, mashed*
1 tablespoon cream	*1 tablespoon cream*

METHOD

Roll the cheese into balls about the size of a walnut. (If cottage cheese is used, it should be sieved first.) Roll the cheese balls in the chopped nuts and chill. Put some shredded escarole, endive or lettuce in four glass serving dishes and arrange the apple slices, scampi or large shrimps (prawns) and cheese balls on top. Combine all the dressing ingredients and pour over the individual salads.

Serves 4.

RAW VEGETABLES WITH HOT GARLIC SAUCE

IMPERIAL/METRIC	AMERICAN
3 oz. (75 grms.) unsalted butter	*$\frac{3}{8}$ cup unsalted butter*
5 tablespoons olive oil	*5 tablespoons olive oil*
1 small can anchovies in oil, chopped	*1 small can anchovies in oil, chopped*
2 to 6 garlic cloves, finely chopped	*2 to 6 garlic cloves, finely chopped*
4 celery stalks, cut into 2 inch (5 cm.) lengths	*4 celery stalks, cut into 2 inch lengths*
1 red pepper, pith and seeds removed, cut into thin strips	*1 red pepper, pith and seeds removed, cut into thin strips*
1 green pepper, pith and seeds removed, cut into thin strips	*1 green pepper, pith and seeds removed, cut into thin strips*
4 small carrots, peeled and cut into sticks	*4 small carrots, peeled and cut into sticks*
$\frac{1}{4}$ small white cabbage, cut into fairly wide strips	*$\frac{1}{4}$ small white cabbage, cut into fairly wide strips*

Raw vegetables with hot garlic sauce

METHOD

Put the butter, olive oil, anchovies (with their oil) and garlic into a saucepan and cook gently, stirring occasionally, for 15 minutes. Transfer to a fondue pot, chafing dish or heatproof dish on a plate warmer and serve with the raw vegetables.

Serves 6 to 8.

Sweetcorn scallops

SWEETCORN SCALLOPS

IMPERIAL/METRIC	AMERICAN
1 × 10 oz. (250 grms.) packet frozen sweetcorn	*1 × 10 oz. packet frozen corn*
1½ oz. (38 grms.) butter or margarine	*3 tablespoons butter or margarine*
1½ oz. (38 grms.) flour	*6 tablespoons flour*
¾ pint (375 ml.) milk	*2 cups milk*
2 tablespoons cream	*2 tablespoons cream*
salt and pepper	*salt and pepper*
pinch of cayenne pepper	*pinch of cayenne pepper*
pinch of grated nutmeg	*pinch of grated nutmeg*
2 oz. (50 grms.) fresh breadcrumbs fried in 1 oz. (25 grms.) butter or margarine until golden	*½ cup fresh breadcrumbs fried in 2 tablespoons butter or margarine until golden*
3 bacon rashers	*3 bacon slices*

METHOD

Cook the sweetcorn according to the directions on the packet. Drain. Melt the butter or margarine and stir in the flour. Cook, stirring, for 1 minute. Gradually add the milk, stirring constantly. Bring to the boil and simmer until the mixture thickens. Stir in the cream, seasoning, cayenne, nutmeg and corn. Divide the mixture between six or eight scallop dishes or shells and sprinkle with the breadcrumbs. Cut each bacon rasher (slice) into three long strips and stretch them using the back of a knife. Roll up the strips and thread on to a metal skewer. Grill (broil) the bacon until it is crisp. Meanwhile, bake the scallops in a moderate oven, 350°F, Gas Mark 4, for 15 to 20 minutes or until heated through. Garnish with the bacon rolls.

Serves 6 to 8.

COURGETTE (ZUCCHINI) SOUP

IMPERIAL/METRIC	AMERICAN
1 lb. (½ kilo) courgettes, sliced	*1 lb. zucchini, sliced*
1½ oz. (38 grms.) butter or margarine	*3 tablespoons butter or margarine*
1 × 15 oz. (375 grms.) can consommé soup	*1 × 15 oz. can consommé soup*
salt and pepper	*salt and pepper*
½ bunch watercress	*½ bunch watercress*
¼ pint (125 ml.) plain yogurt	*⅝ cup plain yogurt*

METHOD

Cook the courgettes (zucchini) gently in the butter or margarine until soft. Add the consommé and seasoning. Discard the thick watercress stalks and add the leaves to the pan. Cover and simmer for 20 minutes. Purée the soup in a liquidiser or with a food mill and chill. Stir in the yogurt just before serving.

Serves 4.

FROSTED TOMATO COCKTAIL

IMPERIAL/METRIC	AMERICAN
2 lb. (1 kilo) tomatoes, skinned and chopped	*2 lb. tomatoes, skinned and chopped*
4 tablespoons water	*4 tablespoons water*
salt and pepper	*salt and pepper*
pinch of sugar	*pinch of sugar*
squeeze of lemon juice	*squeeze of lemon juice*
dash of Worcestershire sauce	*dash of Worcestershire sauce*
mint leaves	*mint leaves*

METHOD

Put the tomatoes, water, seasoning and sugar into a saucepan and heat for a few minutes. Rub through a sieve or purée in a liquidiser. Add lemon juice, Worcestershire sauce and any other seasonings you like, such as celery salt, cayenne pepper or chilli sauce. Put into a freezing tray and freeze slightly. Chop lightly and spoon into chilled glasses. Garnish with mint leaves. **Serves 4 to 6.**

Frosted tomato cocktail

TUNA MOUSSE

IMPERIAL/METRIC	AMERICAN
½ oz. (12½ grms.) butter or margarine	*1 tablespoon butter or margarine*
½ oz. (12½ grms.) flour	*2 tablespoons flour*
¼ pint (125 ml.) milk	*⅝ cup milk*
1 egg, separated	*1 egg, separated*
2 tablespoons chopped capers	*2 tablespoons chopped capers*
1 tablespoon chopped parsley	*1 tablespoon chopped parsley*
1 × 8 oz. (200 grms.) can tuna, drained and flaked	*1 × 8 oz. can tuna, drained and flaked*
½ oz. (12½ grms.) gelatine	*½ oz. gelatin*
¼ pint (125 ml.) hot water	*⅝ cup hot water*
¼ pint (125 ml.) double cream, whipped	*⅝ cup heavy cream, whipped*
lemon juice	*lemon juice*
salt and pepper	*salt and pepper*
gherkins to garnish	*gherkins to garnish*

METHOD

Melt the butter or margarine and stir in the flour. Cook, stirring, for 1 minute. Gradually add the milk, stirring constantly. Bring to the boil and simmer until the mixture has thickened. Remove the pan from the heat and blend in the egg yolk, capers, parsley and tuna. Dissolve the gelatine in the hot water and stir into the fish mixture. Add the cream, with lemon juice and seasoning to taste. Whisk the egg white until it is stiff and fold it carefully into the fish mixture. Put into a dampened mould or basin and chill until set. Turn out and garnish with gherkins. **Serves 6 to 8.**

After-School Snacks

FRESH EGG LEMONADE

IMPERIAL/METRIC	AMERICAN
2 eggs	*2 eggs*
6 fl. oz. (150 ml.) lemon juice	*¾ cup lemon juice*
1 tablespoon castor sugar	*1 tablespoon superfine sugar*
soda water	*soda water*

METHOD

Blend or shake together the eggs, lemon juice and sugar. Taste and add more sugar if you like. Strain into two tall glasses and fill with soda. Top with an ice cube.
Serves 2.

FLAPJACKS

IMPERIAL/METRIC	AMERICAN
4 oz. (100 grms.) butter or margarine	*½ cup butter or margarine*
1 tablespoon brown sugar	*1 tablespoon brown sugar*
4 tablespoons golden syrup	*4 tablespoons light corn syrup*
8 oz. (200 grms.) rolled oats	*2 cups rolled oats*
pinch of salt	*pinch of salt*

METHOD

Melt the butter or margarine with the sugar and syrup. Add the oats and salt and mix well. Spread the mixture smoothly in an 8 × 12 inch (20 × 30 cm.) tin and bake in a moderate oven, 350°F, Gas Mark 4, for 15 to 20 minutes or until golden brown and firm to the touch. Cut into squares or fingers while warm. Cool in the tin.
Makes 18 to 24.

FRENCH TOAST

IMPERIAL/METRIC	AMERICAN
few drops vanilla essence	*few drops vanilla extract*
¼ pint (125 ml.) milk	*⅝ cup milk*
2 slices stale bread, about ½ inch (1¼ cm.) thick	*2 slices stale bread, about ½ inch thick*
1 egg, beaten	*1 egg, beaten*
oil for frying	*oil for frying*
2 tablespoons sugar mixed with a pinch of ground cinnamon	*2 tablespoons sugar mixed with a pinch of ground cinnamon*

METHOD

Mix the vanilla with the milk. Soak the bread in the milk for about 5 minutes. Quickly dip the bread in the beaten egg, using two spoons to turn it, then fry in oil until the bread is crisp and golden brown on both sides. Sprinkle with the sugar mixture.
Serves 2.

Fresh egg lemonade

DATE CRUNCHIES

IMPERIAL/METRIC

4 oz. (100 grms.) wholewheat flour
6 oz. (150 grms.) rolled oats
8 oz. (200 grms.) butter or margarine
8 oz. (200 grms.) dates
2 tablespoons water
1 tablespoon lemon juice
1 tablespoon honey
pinch of ground cinnamon

AMERICAN

1 cup wholewheat flour
$1\frac{1}{2}$ cups rolled oats
1 cup butter or margarine
$1\frac{1}{3}$ cups dates
2 tablespoons water
1 tablespoon lemon juice
1 tablespoon honey
pinch of ground cinnamon

METHOD

Mix together the flour and oats. Add the butter or margarine and rub in well. Divide the mixture in half and press one-half in the bottom of a greased 7-inch ($17\frac{1}{2}$-cm.) square cake tin.

Simmer the dates with the water until soft. Cool and stir in the lemon juice, honey and cinnamon. Spread the date mixture over the oat mixture and cover with the remaining oat mixture. Smooth the top. Bake in a moderate oven, 350°F, Gas Mark 4, for 25 minutes. Cut into fingers while still warm. Cool in the tin.

Makes 14.

Scotch pancakes

SCOTCH PANCAKES

IMPERIAL/METRIC

4 oz. (100 grms.) self-raising flour
pinch of salt
1 egg
$\frac{1}{4}$ pint (125 ml.) milk or mixed milk and water
fat for frying

AMERICAN

1 cup self-rising flour
pinch of salt
1 egg
$\frac{5}{8}$ cup milk or mixed milk and water
fat for frying

METHOD

Sift the flour and salt into a bowl. Add the egg and beat well, then gradually beat in the milk or milk and water to give a smooth batter. To cook the pancakes, use a griddle (sometimes called a girdle or bakestone), solid hotplate on an electric cooker (stove), or a heavy-based frying-pan. Grease the griddle or substitute and heat. Test by dropping a teaspoon of the batter on to the griddle; it should begin to set at once and start to bubble within 1 minute if the griddle is hot enough. Drop the batter from a tablespoon on to the griddle and cook for 1 to 2 minutes until the top is covered with bubbles. Turn and cook the other side. Serve warm or cold.

Makes 10 to 12.

B *is for . . .* BREAKFASTS AND BRUNCHES: *begin your day with a sustaining dish– eggs in different guises or a Russian favourite . . .*
BUFFET FOOD: *enjoy entertaining in a way that lets you spend time with your guests, and not in the kitchen*

Breakfasts and Brunches

Piroshki

PIROSHKI

IMPERIAL/METRIC	AMERICAN
Batter	Batter
4 oz. (100 grms.) flour	*1 cup flour*
pinch of salt	*pinch of salt*
1 egg	*1 egg*
½ pint (250 ml.) milk	*1¼ cups milk*
oil for frying	*oil for frying*
egg white	*egg white*
deep fat for frying	*deep fat for frying*
Filling	Filling
8 oz. (200 grms.) cream or cottage cheese	*8 oz. cream or cottage cheese*
1 oz. (25 grms.) butter or margarine	*2 tablespoons butter or margarine*
1 egg	*1 egg*
salt and pepper	*salt and pepper*

METHOD
Sift the flour and salt into a bowl. Add the egg and milk and mix to a smooth thin batter. Use two-thirds of the batter to make eight pancakes (crêpes). Whisk the egg white and fold into the remaining batter.

Mix together the filling ingredients. Put the filling into the centres of the pancakes, roll them up and tuck in the ends to make secure parcels. Dip each parcel in the remaining batter and deep fry until golden brown.
Serves 4.

EGGS EN COCOTTE

IMPERIAL/METRIC	AMERICAN
butter or margarine	*butter or margarine*
salt and pepper	*salt and pepper*
8 eggs	*8 eggs*
4 tablespoons cream	*4 tablespoons cream*

METHOD

Grease four individual ovenproof cocotte dishes with butter or margarine and sprinkle with salt and pepper. Break 2 eggs into each dish. Top with a piece of butter or margarine and 1 tablespoon cream each. Place the dishes in a baking dish of hot water and bake in a moderate oven, 350°F, Gas Mark 4, for 8 to 10 minutes or until the eggs are set.

Serves 4.

BAKED EGGS AND HAM WITH MUSHROOMS

IMPERIAL/METRIC	AMERICAN
4 oz. (100 grms.) sliced lean cooked ham	*4 oz. sliced lean cooked ham*
1 × 10 oz. (250 grms.) can mushrooms, drained	*1 × 10 oz. can mushrooms, drained*
salt and pepper	*salt and pepper*
4 eggs	*4 eggs*

METHOD

Put the ham and mushrooms into a greased baking dish or tin. Season. Cover the dish with foil and bake in a moderately hot oven, 400°F, Gas Mark 6, for 10 minutes. Break the eggs over the ham, return the dish to the oven and bake for a further 10 minutes or until the whites of the eggs are set.

Serves 2.

NOVA SCOTIA EGGS

IMPERIAL/METRIC	AMERICAN
4 eggs	*4 eggs*
4 thin slices smoked salmon	*4 thin slices smoked salmon*
juice of 1 lemon	*juice of 1 lemon*
8 tablespoons thick mayonnaise	*8 tablespoons thick mayonnaise*
shredded lettuce	*shredded lettuce*
lemon slices	*lemon slices*
tomato slices	*tomato slices*

METHOD

Place the eggs carefully in a pan of boiling water and simmer for 5 minutes. Plunge into a bowl of cold water and when cold remove the shells.

Lay a slice of smoked salmon on the centre of each of four small serving plates. Sprinkle with lemon juice. Place an egg in the centre of each and coat neatly with 2 tablespoons mayonnaise. Surround with shredded lettuce and garnish with lemon and tomato slices.

Serves 4.

Eggs en cocotte

Buffet Food

Cold loin of pork orientale

EGG MOUSSE

IMPERIAL/METRIC

6 hard-boiled eggs, finely chopped
1 tablespoon very finely chopped onion
1 tablespoon chopped parsley
$\frac{1}{2}$ teaspoon anchovy essence
4 heaped tablespoons mayonnaise
$\frac{1}{4}$ pint (125 ml.) soured cream or yogurt
1 × 10 oz. (250 grms.) can consommé soup
2 teaspoons gelatine
2 tablespoons warm water
salt and pepper

AMERICAN

6 hard-boiled eggs, finely chopped
1 tablespoon very finely chopped onion
1 tablespoon chopped parsley
$\frac{1}{2}$ teaspoon anchovy paste
4 heaped tablespoons mayonnaise
$\frac{5}{8}$ cup sour cream or yogurt
1 × 10 oz. can consommé soup
2 teaspoons gelatin
2 tablespoons warm water
salt and pepper

METHOD

Mix together the eggs, onion, parsley, anchovy essence (paste), mayonnaise, soured cream or yogurt and two-thirds of the can of soup. Dissolve the gelatine in the water and stir into the egg mixture. Season to taste. Turn into a serving dish and chill. Chill the remaining consommé and when it is set like a jelly, chop it and use to decorate the mousse.
Serves 6 to 8.

COLD LOIN OF PORK ORIENTALE

IMPERIAL/METRIC

1 × 5 lb. (2$\frac{1}{2}$ kilos) loin of pork, boned and rolled
dry mustard
4 fl. oz. (100 ml.) plus 2 tablespoons sherry
4 fl. oz. (100 ml.) plus 2 tablespoons soya sauce
1 tablespoon grated fresh ginger or 2 teaspoons ground ginger
2 garlic cloves, crushed
8 oz. (200 grms.) red currant jelly

AMERICAN

1 × 5 lb. loin of pork, boned and rolled
dry mustard
$\frac{1}{2}$ cup plus 2 tablespoons sherry
$\frac{1}{2}$ cup plus 2 tablespoons soy sauce
1 tablespoon grated fresh ginger or 2 tablespoons ground ginger
2 garlic cloves, crushed
8 oz. red currant jelly

METHOD

Rub the pork with mustard. Mix together the 4 fl. oz. (100 ml.) or $\frac{1}{2}$ cup each of sherry and soya sauce, the ginger and garlic. Pour this mixture over the pork and leave to marinate for 2 hours, turning occasionally. Place the pork on a rack in a roasting pan and roast in a moderate oven, 350°F, Gas Mark 4, for 2$\frac{1}{2}$ to 3 hours or until the meat is cooked. Baste with the marinade from time to time during the roasting.

Melt the red currant jelly in a saucepan. Stir in the remaining 2 tablespoons each of sherry and soya sauce and heat for 1 minute. Spoon this mixture over the pork and leave in a cold place. Serve at room temperature.
Serves 8 to 10.

Salmon trout in aspic

SALMON TROUT IN ASPIC

IMPERIAL/METRIC	AMERICAN
1 × 3 to 4 lb. (1½ to 2 kilo) salmon trout	*1 × 3 to 4 lb. salmon trout*
2 egg whites	*2 egg whites*
2 oz. (50 grms.) gelatine	*2 oz. gelatin*
3 tablespoons sherry	*3 tablespoons sherry*
prawns, cucumber and lemon slices for garnish	*shrimps, cucumber and lemon slices for garnish*
green and black olives for garnish	*green and black olives for garnish*
Court bouillon	Court bouillon
2 pints (1 l.) water	*5 cups water*
½ pint (250 ml.) white wine	*1¼ cups white wine*
1 onion, sliced	*1 onion, sliced*
2 shallots, chopped	*2 shallots, chopped*
bouquet garni	*bouquet garni*
1 teaspoon salt	*1 teaspoon salt*
6 white peppercorns	*6 white peppercorns*

METHOD
First make the court bouillon. Place all the ingredients in a saucepan, cover and bring to the boil. Simmer for 30 minutes and strain.

Wash the trout, clean the cavities and rub with salt. Rinse well. Curl the trout and place it in a deep oven-proof dish. Pour over the court bouillon and cover with a lid or aluminium foil, making sure it doesn't touch the fish. Bake in a moderately low oven, 325°F, Gas Mark 3, for 40 to 50 minutes, basting frequently. Cool in the court bouillon.

Remove the skin from the trout. Make a cut on either side of the backbone, snip at each end and remove the backbone carefully.

Measure the court bouillon and make up to 2 pints (1 l.) or 5 cups with water or mixed white wine and water. Put into a saucepan, preferably an enamel or tin-lined pan. Add the egg whites and gelatine and whisk with a wire or balloon whisk. Bring slowly to the boil, whisking constantly. Remove from the heat and leave for 20 minutes. Strain through a scalded jelly bag or cloth. Stir in the sherry and allow this aspic to cool.

Spoon the aspic carefully over the cooked salmon trout until it is glazed with a thin layer. Pour a thin layer of aspic on to the bottom of a serving platter and allow to set. Very carefully lift the fish on to the serving platter. Garnish with chopped aspic, prawns (shrimps), cucumber and lemon slices and olives.

Serves 6.

French apple flan

FRENCH APPLE FLAN

IMPERIAL/METRIC

Pastry

8 oz. (200 grms.) flour
pinch of salt
4 oz. (100 grms.) butter or margarine
1 egg
water

Filling

2 lb. (1 kilo) cooking apples, peeled, cored and quartered
¼ pint (125 ml.) white wine
strip of lemon rind
2 oz. (50 grms.) butter or margarine
4 oz. (100 grms.) sugar
4 crisp eating apples, peeled, cored and thinly sliced
3 tablespoons apricot jam
1 tablespoon lemon juice

AMERICAN

Pastry

2 cups flour
pinch of salt
½ cup butter or margarine
1 egg
water

Filling

2 lb. cooking apples, peeled, cored and quartered
⅝ cup white wine
strip of lemon rind
¼ cup butter or margarine
½ cup sugar
4 crisp eating apples, peeled, cored and thinly sliced
3 tablespoons apricot jam
1 tablespoon lemon juice

METHOD

First make the pastry. Sift the flour and salt into a bowl. Add the butter or margarine and rub in until the mixture resembles breadcrumbs. Mix in the egg and enough water to make a smooth dough. Chill for 30 minutes.

Meanwhile, put the cooking apples, wine, lemon rind, butter or margarine and half the sugar in a saucepan. Cover and simmer gently until the apples are tender. Remove the lemon rind and purée the apple mixture in a liquidiser or by pushing through a sieve.

Roll out the dough into a circle large enough to line an 8 inch (20 cm.) diameter flan ring (standing on a baking sheet) or shallow cake tin. Trim off any excess dough. Put the apple purée in the flan case. Arrange the eating apple slices, overlapping, on top of the apple purée. Sprinkle with the remaining sugar and bake in a moderately hot oven, 375°F, Gas Mark 5, for 25 to 30 minutes or until the apples are tender and the pastry is golden.

Melt the jam with the lemon juice in a saucepan. Sieve and glaze the hot cooked flan with the apricot mixture.

Serves 6.

C *is for . . .* CHILDREN'S FAVOURITES: *you can't beat these kid-tempters that are quick to make, with a super and amusing cake for a party, too . . .*
COST-SAVERS: *as budgets get tighter and prices go up, make the most of the food you buy*

Children's Favourites

SAUSAGE BOATS

IMPERIAL/METRIC	AMERICAN
6 to 8 large sausages	*6 to 8 large sausages*
6 to 8 very thin slices bread	*6 to 8 very thin slices bread*
butter or margarine	*butter or margarine*
watercress and tomatoes	*watercress and tomatoes*

METHOD
Grill (broil) or fry the sausages until they are cooked. Spread one side of each bread slice with butter or margarine. Put a sausage in the centre and gather up the sides to form a boat shape. Secure with wooden cocktail sticks. Brush the outside of the boats with melted butter or margarine. Crisp in a hot oven, 425°F, Gas Mark 7. Garnish with watercress and tomatoes.
Serves 4 to 6.

Sausage boats

MUSHROOM CAKE

IMPERIAL/METRIC	AMERICAN
3 oz. (75 grms.) plain chocolate	*3 oz. (3 squares) semi-sweet chocolate*
2 tablespoons milk	*2 tablespoons milk*
5 oz. (125 grms.) self-raising flour	*$1\frac{1}{4}$ cups self-rising flour*
pinch of salt	*pinch of salt*
4 oz. (100 grms.) butter or margarine	*$\frac{1}{2}$ cup butter or margarine*
4 oz. (100 grms.) castor sugar	*$\frac{1}{2}$ cup superfine sugar*
2 eggs	*2 eggs*
Almond paste	Almond paste
4 oz. (100 grms.) ground almonds	*$\frac{2}{3}$ cup ground almonds*
2 oz. (50 grms.) icing sugar, sifted	*$\frac{1}{3}$ cup confectioners' sugar, sifted*
2 tablespoons castor sugar	*2 tablespoons superfine sugar*
squeeze of lemon juice	*squeeze of lemon juice*
1 egg yolk	*1 egg yolk*
1 tablespoon warmed apricot jam, sieved	*1 tablespoon warmed apricot jam, sieved*
Cream topping	Cream topping
2 oz. (50 grms.) butter or margarine	*$\frac{1}{4}$ cup butter or margarine*
4 oz. (100 grms.) icing sugar, sifted	*$\frac{2}{3}$ cup confectioners' sugar, sifted*
1 oz. (25 grms.) plain chocolate, melted in 2 teaspoons hot milk	*1 oz. (1 square) semi-sweet chocolate, melted in 2 teaspoons hot milk*

METHOD

Gently melt the chocolate in the milk. Cool. Sift the flour and salt together. Cream the butter or margarine with the sugar until light and fluffy, then beat in the eggs one at a time with a spoonful of flour each. Mix in the chocolate milk mixture with another spoonful of flour. Gently fold in the remaining flour. Spoon the batter into a greased and lined 8 inch (20 cm.) deep cake tin. Bake in a moderately hot oven, 375°F, Gas Mark 5, for 30 to 40 minutes or until well risen and firm. Cool on a wire cake rack.

To make the almond paste, mix together the almonds, sugars, lemon juice and egg yolk. Turn on to a sugared surface and knead. Roll out into a 10 inch (25 cm.) circle. Brush with jam and place the cake in the centre. Press the almond paste against the sides of the cake and trim away the excess. Roll the trimmings to form a 'stalk'.

To make the cream topping, cream together the butter or margarine and sugar, then gradually beat in the melted chocolate. Beat well and chill until the cream is firm. Pipe or spread on top of the cake, marking into grooves with a fork to resemble a mushroom. Put the 'stalk' in the centre.

Serves 8 to 10.

Mushroom cake

FRUIT QUEEN OF PUDDINGS

IMPERIAL/METRIC	AMERICAN
2 tablespoons jam	*2 tablespoons jam*
2 oz. (50 grms.) soft fresh breadcrumbs	*½ cup soft fresh breadcrumbs*
¾ pint (375 ml.) milk	*2 cups milk*
2 eggs, separated	*2 eggs, separated*
3 oz. (75 grms.) castor sugar	*⅜ cup superfine sugar*
3 tablespoons diced fresh or canned fruit	*3 tablespoons diced fresh or canned fruit*

METHOD

Spread half the jam in an ovenproof dish. Add the crumbs. Heat the milk but do not let it boil. Mix together the egg yolks and one-third of the sugar. Pour on the hot milk, stirring constantly. Strain this custard on to the breadcrumbs. Spread with the remaining jam and most of the fruit. Whip the egg whites until stiff, then fold in the remaining sugar. Pile on to the custard mixture and top with the remaining fruit. Bake in a moderate oven, 350°F, Gas Mark 4, for 15 minutes.

Serves 4.

APPLE BAKE

IMPERIAL/METRIC	AMERICAN
2 lb. (1 kilo) cooking apples, peeled, cored and sliced	*2 lb. cooking apples, peeled, cored and sliced*
2 tablespoons water	*2 tablespoons water*
6 tablespoons brown sugar	*6 tablespoons brown sugar*
2 oz. (50 grms.) cornflakes	*2 cups cornflakes*
2 tablespoons desiccated coconut	*2 tablespoons shredded coconut*
grated rind of 1 lemon	*grated rind of 1 lemon*
1 oz. (25 grms.) butter or margarine	*2 tablespoons butter or margarine*

METHOD

Put the apples in a saucepan with the water and 4 tablespoons of the sugar. Cover and simmer gently until the apples are soft. Turn into four small ovenproof dishes. Mix together the cornflakes, coconut, remaining sugar and the lemon rind. Sprinkle over the apples. Dot with butter or margarine. Bake in a moderately hot oven, 375°F, Gas Mark 5, for 20 minutes.

Serves 4.

Cost Savers

CHILLI CON CARNE

IMPERIAL/METRIC	AMERICAN
1 onion, chopped	*1 onion, chopped*
1 garlic clove, crushed	*1 garlic clove, crushed*
2 tablespoons oil	*2 tablespoons oil*
1 lb. (½ kilo) lean minced beef	*1 lb. lean ground beef*
1 small green pepper, pith and seeds removed, chopped	*1 small green pepper, pith and seeds removed, chopped*
1 × 15 oz. (375 grms.) can tomatoes	*1 × 15 oz. can tomatoes*
1 pint (½ l.) water	*2½ cups water*
1 bay leaf	*1 bay leaf*
½ teaspoon chilli powder	*½ teaspoon chilli powder*
pinch of dried basil	*pinch of dried basil*
salt and pepper	*salt and pepper*
1 × 12 oz. (300 grms.) can red kidney beans, drained	*1 × 12 oz. can red kidney beans, drained*

METHOD

Fry the onion and garlic in the oil until soft. Add the beef and green pepper and fry until the meat is browned. Add all the other ingredients except the kidney beans and bring to the boil. Simmer gently, uncovered, for 30 minutes or until the mixture is quite thick. Stir in the beans, cover and simmer for a further 30 minutes.

Serves 4.

Chilli con carne

TAGLIATELLE WITH BACON AND TOMATO SAUCE

IMPERIAL/METRIC

8 oz. (200 grms.) lean bacon, diced
3 oz. (75 grms.) butter or margarine
1 carrot, diced
4 celery stalks, chopped
1 garlic clove, finely chopped
4 tablespoons tomato paste
4 fl. oz. (100 ml.) water
1 chicken stock cube, crumbled
salt and pepper
8 to 12 oz. (200 to 300 grms.) tagliatelle
grated Parmesan cheese

AMERICAN

8 oz. lean bacon, diced
$\frac{3}{8}$ cup butter or margarine
1 carrot, diced
4 celery stalks, chopped
1 garlic clove, finely chopped
4 tablespoons tomato paste
$\frac{1}{2}$ cup water
1 chicken stock cube, crumbled
salt and pepper
8 to 12 oz. tagliatelle
grated Parmesan cheese

Tagliatelle with bacon and tomato sauce

METHOD

Gently fry the bacon in two-thirds of the butter or margarine. Add the carrot, celery and garlic, cover and simmer for 5 minutes, shaking the pan occasionally. Stir in the tomato paste, water, stock cube and seasoning. Cook gently for a further 5 minutes. Keep hot.

Cook the tagliatelle in boiling salted water for 15 to 20 minutes or until tender. Drain and return to the pan with the remaining butter or margarine. Toss to coat the tagliatelle with the butter or margarine. Sprinkle over some Parmesan cheese and stir gently. Transfer to a warm serving dish and pour the hot bacon and tomato sauce over the top.

Serves 4 to 6.

OXTAIL CASSEROLE

IMPERIAL/METRIC

3 lb. ($1\frac{1}{2}$ kilos) oxtail, in pieces, trimmed of excess fat
2 oz. (50 grms.) lard or dripping
2 onions, chopped
2 large carrots, chopped
$\frac{1}{2}$ head of celery, chopped
2 streaky bacon rashers, chopped
2 tablespoons flour
2 bay leaves
3 parsley sprigs
6 peppercorns
salt
2 pints (1 l.) beef stock
gravy browning

AMERICAN

3 lb. oxtail, in pieces, trimmed of excess fat
$\frac{1}{4}$ cup lard or dripping
2 onions, chopped
2 large carrots, chopped
$\frac{1}{2}$ head of celery, chopped
2 fatty bacon slices, chopped
2 tablespoons flour
2 bay leaves
3 parsley sprigs
6 peppercorns
salt
5 cups beef stock
gravy browning

METHOD

Brown the oxtail quickly on all sides in the lard or dripping. Remove from the pan. Add the vegetables and bacon to the pan and cook gently for 5 minutes. Blend in the flour and cook, stirring, for 1 minute. Return the oxtail to the pan with the remaining ingredients except for the gravy browning. Cover and simmer for 4 hours or until the meat is falling off the bones. Arrange the meat on a serving dish and keep hot. Boil the cooking liquid until it has reduced to about $\frac{3}{4}$ pint (450 ml.) or 2 cups. Strain over the oxtail.

Serves 6.

D *is for . . .* DRINKS AND DIPS: *whether you are planning a large celebration or a small gathering, offer your guests some unusual fare from this selection*

Drinks and Dips

GRENADINE GRAPE

IMPERIAL/METRIC	AMERICAN
$\frac{1}{2}$ pint (250 ml.) grape juice	*$1\frac{1}{4}$ cups grape juice*
1 tablespoon grenadine	*1 tablespoon grenadine*
1 egg white	*1 egg white*
soda	*soda*

METHOD

Thoroughly shake the grape juice, grenadine and egg white with crushed ice. Strain into two tall glasses and fill with soda.

Serves 2.

TEA PUNCH

IMPERIAL/METRIC	AMERICAN
$\frac{1}{2}$ pint (250 ml.) peach juice	*$1\frac{1}{4}$ cups peach juice*
2 pints (1 l.) orange juice	*5 cups orange juice*
1 pint ($\frac{1}{2}$ l.) strong tea	*$2\frac{1}{2}$ cups strong tea*
2 teaspoons orange bitters	*2 teaspoons orange bitters*
2 large bottles dry ginger ale	*2 large bottles dry ginger ale*
orange slices to garnish	*orange slices to garnish*

METHOD

Pour the fruit juices and tea over a large block of ice in a punch bowl. Add the orange bitters and dry ginger ale. Garnish with orange slices.

Serves 15.

WHITE WINE PUNCH

IMPERIAL/METRIC	AMERICAN
8 oz. (200 grms.) cherries, stoned	*8 oz. cherries, stoned*
1 lb. ($\frac{1}{2}$ kilo) fresh pineapple cubes	*1 lb. fresh pineapple cubes*
4 fl. oz. (100 ml.) kirsch	*$\frac{1}{2}$ cup kirsch*
2 oz. (50 grms.) castor sugar	*$\frac{1}{4}$ cup superfine sugar*
1 bottle dry white wine	*1 bottle dry white wine*
6 dashes orange bitters	*6 dashes orange bitters*
1 pint ($\frac{1}{2}$ l.) pineapple juice	*$2\frac{1}{2}$ cups pineapple juice*

METHOD

Marinate the cherries and pineapple cubes in the kirsch and sugar overnight. Mix with the remaining ingredients in a large punch bowl. Add crushed ice. Serve in tall glasses topped up with soda.

Serves 10 to 12.

Grenadine grape

Fruit juices

FRUIT JUICES

IMPERIAL/METRIC	AMERICAN
fruit, such as damsons, black cherries, black and red currants, strawberries, raspberries, loganberries, etc.	*fruit, such as damsons, black cherries, black and red currants, strawberries, raspberries, loganberries, etc.*
water if necessary	*water if necessary*
sugar	*sugar*

METHOD

Wash and drain the fruit. Place it in a large heatproof bowl over a saucepan of simmering water. If currants are being used, add ½ pint (250 ml.) or 1¼ cups water for each 1 lb. (½ kilo) of fruit; blackberries will need ½ pint (250 ml.) or 1¼ cups water for each 6 lb. (3 kilo) of fruit. The other fruits need no water. Keep the water in the saucepan simmering all the time, adding more boiling water as necessary. Cook the fruit until the juices start to flow – this will take about 1 hour. Press the fruit occasionally with a wooden spoon. Pour the pulp and juice into a scalded jelly bag and allow the juice to strain through overnight into a bowl. Do not press or squeeze the bag or the juice will be cloudy. Measure the juice and return it to the bowl over the saucepan of simmering water. Add 3 oz. (75 grms.) or ⅜ cup sugar for each pint (½ l.) or 2½ cups of juice. Stir to dissolve the sugar. Pour into clean bottles and seal. Place the bottles upright in a deep pan with a false bottom and support them with strips of newspaper. Add enough boiling water to come above the level of the juice. Maintain the water at simmering point for 20 minutes. Remove the bottles from the pan and screw down the tops or press the corks in again firmly.

GUACAMOLE

IMPERIAL/METRIC

2 large avocado pears
3 large tomatoes, skinned
1 small onion, finely chopped
$\frac{1}{4}$ pint (125 ml.) soured cream
1 tablespoon lemon juice
3 tablespoons mayonnaise
salt and pepper
few drops Tabasco sauce

AMERICAN

2 large avocados
3 large tomatoes, skinned
1 small onion, finely chopped
$\frac{5}{8}$ cup sour cream
1 tablespoon lemon juice
3 tablespoons mayonnaise
salt and pepper
few drops Tabasco sauce

METHOD

Halve the avocados and remove the stones. Scoop out the flesh and mash with all the remaining ingredients. Serve with crisps (potato chips), raw vegetables and biscuits (crackers).

Serves 10 to 12.

Guacamole

Taramasalata

TARAMASALATA

IMPERIAL/METRIC	AMERICAN
8 oz. (200 grms.) smoked cod's roe	*8 oz. smoked cod's roe*
2 oz. (50 grms.) butter or margarine or 2 tablespoons olive oil	*¼ cup butter or margarine or 2 tablespoons olive oil*
lemon juice	*lemon juice*
pepper	*pepper*
1 garlic clove, crushed	*1 garlic clove, crushed*
chopped parsley	*chopped parsley*

METHOD

Remove the skin from the roe. Blend the roe with the butter or margarine or oil, lemon juice to taste, pepper and garlic. Put into a bowl and top with parsley. Serve with hot toast, lemon and butter.

Serves 4 to 6.

COTTAGE CHEESE DIPS

Blend an 8 ounce (200 grms.) carton of cottage cheese with chopped prunes; or with crushed garlic and caraway seeds; or with crushed garlic and chopped chives. Serve with carrot and celery sticks.

CHEESE STRAWS

IMPERIAL/METRIC	AMERICAN
8 oz. (200 grms.) flour	*2 cups flour*
pinch of salt	*pinch of salt*
shake of pepper	*shake of pepper*
pinch of cayenne pepper	*pinch of cayenne pepper*
pinch of dry mustard	*pinch of dry mustard*
4 oz. (100 grms.) butter or margarine	*½ cup butter or margarine*
3 oz. (75 grms.) Parmesan cheese, grated	*¾ cup grated Parmesan cheese*
2 egg yolks	*2 egg yolks*
water	*water*
egg white	*egg white*

METHOD

Sift the flour, salt, pepper, cayenne and mustard into a bowl. Rub the butter or margarine into the dry ingredients until the mixture resembles breadcrumbs. Mix in the cheese, then the egg yolks with enough water to make a firm dough. Roll out the dough to about ⅓ inch (¾ cm.) thickness. Cut into narrow fingers and put these on well greased baking sheets. Save a little dough to make rings. Brush the fingers and rings with egg white and bake in a hot oven, 425°F, Gas Mark 7, for 8 to 10 minutes. Cool. To serve, put some of the straws through the rings.

Makes about 60 straws and 8 to 10 rings.

Cheese strau

E *is for . . .* EASY ENOUGH FOR BEGINNERS:
even first-time cooks can make these simple yet interesting dishes – salad, entrée, dessert and savoury snack

Easy Enough for Beginners

Crab and tomato toasts

CRAB AND TOMATO TOASTS

IMPERIAL/METRIC	AMERICAN
4 circles of bread	*4 circles of bread*
2 oz. (50 grms.) butter or margarine	*¼ cup butter or margarine*
juice of ½ lemon	*juice of ½ lemon*
1 × 7 oz. (175 grms.) can crabmeat	*1 × 7 oz. can crabmeat*
salt and pepper	*salt and pepper*
1 tablespoon tomato paste	*1 tablespoon tomato paste*
watercress	*watercress*
lemon slices	*lemon slices*

METHOD

Toast the bread and spread with half the butter or margarine. Keep hot. Mix together the lemon juice, crabmeat, seasoning, tomato paste and the rest of the butter or margarine. Spread on to the hot toast. Heat under the grill (broiler) for a few minutes. Garnish with the watercress and lemon slices.

Serves 4.

TOMATO SALAD WITH ORANGE

IMPERIAL/METRIC	AMERICAN
1 lb. (½ kilo) tomatoes	*1 lb. tomatoes*
2 oranges, peeled and segmented	*2 oranges, peeled and segmented*
3 tablespoons olive oil	*3 tablespoons olive oil*
1 tablespoon wine vinegar	*1 tablespoon wine vinegar*
1 teaspoon sugar	*1 teaspoon sugar*
½ teaspoon dry mustard	*½ teaspoon dry mustard*
salt and pepper	*salt and pepper*
1 garlic clove, finely chopped	*1 garlic clove, finely chopped*
1 tablespoon chopped fresh basil or 1 teaspoon dried basil	*1 tablespoon chopped fresh basil or 1 teaspoon dried basil*
finely grated rind of 1 lemon	*finely grated rind of 1 lemon*

METHOD

Thinly slice the tomatoes or cut them into wedges. Arrange them in a flat shallow dish with the orange segments. Mix together the remaining ingredients and pour this dressing over the tomatoes and oranges. Chill for 30 minutes.

Serves 4 to 6.

DEVILLED CHICKEN

IMPERIAL/METRIC	AMERICAN
3 tablespoons chutney	*3 tablespoons chutney*
1 tablespoon tomato paste	*1 tablespoon tomato paste*
$\frac{1}{4}$ teaspoon Tabasco sauce	*$\frac{1}{4}$ teaspoon Tabasco sauce*
$\frac{1}{4}$ teaspoon prepared mustard	*$\frac{1}{4}$ teaspoon prepared mustard*
salt and pepper	*salt and pepper*
4 chicken pieces	*4 chicken pieces*

METHOD
Mix together the chutney, tomato paste, Tabasco sauce, mustard and seasoning. Place the chicken in a roasting tin and spoon over the chutney mixture. Cover with foil and roast in a moderately hot oven, 400°F, Gas Mark 6, for 45 minutes. Uncover and continue roasting for a further 10 to 15 minutes or until the chicken is tender.
Serves 4.

BRAISED BEEF NEAPOLITAN

IMPERIAL/METRIC	AMERICAN
4×6 to 8 oz. (150 to 200 grms.) braising steaks	*4×6 to 8 oz. braising steaks*
salt and pepper	*salt and pepper*
1 lb. ($\frac{1}{2}$ kilo) tomatoes, skinned and chopped	*1 lb. tomatoes, skinned and chopped*
1 onion, chopped	*1 onion, chopped*
1 garlic clove, crushed	*1 garlic clove, crushed*
1 bay leaf	*1 bay leaf*
$\frac{1}{2}$ teaspoon mixed dried herbs	*$\frac{1}{2}$ teaspoon mixed dried herbs*

METHOD
Season the steaks and grill (broil) them for 5 minutes on each side. Mix together the remaining ingredients. Place the steaks in a casserole and spoon over the tomato mixture. Braise in a moderate oven, 350°F, Gas Mark 4, for 1 to 2 hours, depending on the quality of the meat.
Serves 4.

CORNFLAKE BROWN BETTY

IMPERIAL/METRIC	AMERICAN
5 oz. (125 grms.) cornflakes	*4 cups cornflakes*
3 oz. (75 grms.) butter or margarine, melted	*$\frac{3}{8}$ cup butter or margarine, melted*
2 oz. (50 grms.) brown sugar	*$\frac{1}{3}$ cup brown sugar*
1 lb. ($\frac{1}{2}$ kilo) fruit, such as raspberries	*1 lb. fruit, such as raspberries*

METHOD
Gently mix together the cornflakes, butter or margarine and brown sugar. Put one-third of this mixture into a pie or ovenproof dish and spoon over half the fruit. Cover with another layer of the cornflake mixture and the rest of the fruit. Finish with a layer of the cornflake mixture. Bake in a moderate oven, 350°F, Gas Mark 4, for 35 to 40 minutes. Decorate with more fruit, if you like. If you use firm fruit, such as apples, plums, etc., cook them first in a covered saucepan with a little water and sugar to taste until softened.
Serves 4 to 6.

Devilled chicken

F is for . . . FROZEN FOOD: *a new slant on how to use convenient frozen pastry, vegetables, fish and chicken that you can buy in the supermarket . . .*
FINISHING WITH FLAIR: *desserts that will impress and delight the most discerning palate*

Frozen Food Shortcuts

American salad

AMERICAN SALAD

IMPERIAL/METRIC	AMERICAN
8 oz. (100 grms.) frozen green beans	*8 oz. frozen green beans*
8 oz. (100 grms.) frozen sweetcorn	*8 oz. frozen corn*
1 red pepper, pith and seeds removed, finely diced	*1 red pepper, pith and seeds removed, finely diced*
4 oz. (100 grms.) mushrooms, sliced	*4 oz. mushrooms, sliced*
4 tomatoes, sliced	*4 tomatoes, sliced*
12 black olives, stoned	*12 black olives, stoned*
4 tablespoons olive oil	*4 tablespoons olive oil*
1 tablespoon wine vinegar	*1 tablespoon wine vinegar*
1 tablespoon lemon juice	*1 tablespoon lemon juice*
salt and pepper	*salt and pepper*
1 onion, sliced and pushed out into rings	*1 onion, sliced and pushed out into rings*

METHOD

Cook the beans and corn according to the directions on the packets. When cool, mix together with the red pepper, mushrooms, tomatoes, olives, oil, vinegar and lemon juice. Season well and transfer to a serving dish. Garnish with the onion rings.

Serves 4.

LAMB CUTLETS (CHOPS) IN PASTRY

IMPERIAL/METRIC	AMERICAN
6 large lamb cutlets	*6 large lamb chops*
2 oz. (50 grms.) butter or margarine	*$\frac{1}{4}$ cup butter or margarine*
salt and pepper	*salt and pepper*
2 tomatoes, skinned and chopped	*2 tomatoes, skinned and chopped*
6 oz. (150 grms.) mushrooms, very finely chopped or minced	*6 oz. mushrooms, very finely chopped or ground*
4 oz. (100 grms.) cooked ham, very finely chopped or minced	*4 oz. cooked ham, very finely chopped or ground*
1 tablespoon chopped parsley	*1 tablespoon chopped parsley*
1 × 14 oz. (350 grms.) packet frozen puff pastry, thawed	*1 × 14 oz. packet frozen puff pastry, thawed*
2 egg yolks mixed with 2 tablespoons water	*2 egg yolks mixed with 2 tablespoons water*

METHOD

Dot the cutlets with half the butter or margarine and season. Grill (broil) on both sides until tender. Meanwhile, mix together the tomatoes, mushrooms, ham and parsley. Melt the remaining butter or margarine and add to the tomato mixture. Roll out the pastry dough and cut into six rectangles large enough to enclose the cutlets. Put a spoonful of the tomato mixture on each piece of pastry dough. Place a cutlet on this and top with another spoonful of the tomato mixture. Fold the dough around the cutlet to make a parcel. Place on a baking sheet, joins underneath. Use any trimmings to make decorations. Brush well with the egg yolk mixture and bake in a hot oven, 425°F, Gas Mark 7, for about 20 minutes or until the pastry is golden brown.
Serves 6.

FISH AND BACON WHIRLS

IMPERIAL/METRIC	AMERICAN
8 frozen fish fingers, in breadcrumb coating	*8 frozen fish fingers, in breadcrumb coating*
oil or fat for frying	*oil or fat for frying*
8 streaky bacon rashers, cut into long strips	*8 fat bacon slices, cut into long strips*
4 tomatoes, halved	*4 tomatoes, halved*

METHOD

Fry the fish fingers in oil or fat until golden brown but not quite cooked. Remove them from the pan and wrap the bacon strips around them. Secure them with cocktail sticks if necessary. Return to the pan with the tomatoes and continue frying until the bacon and fish fingers are cooked.
Serves 4.

CHICKEN CORDON BLEU

IMPERIAL/METRIC	AMERICAN
4 frozen chicken breasts, thawed	*4 frozen chicken breasts, thawed*
4 slices cooked ham	*4 slices cooked ham*
4 slices Gruyère cheese	*4 slices Gruyère cheese*
salt and pepper	*salt and pepper*
2 tablespoons flour	*2 tablespoons flour*
Coating	Coating
1 egg, beaten	*1 egg, beaten*
2 oz. (50 grms.) dry breadcrumbs	*$\frac{2}{3}$ cup dry breadcrumbs*
oil or fat for frying	*oil or fat for frying*

METHOD

Dry the chicken breasts well, then slit each to make a pocket. Insert the ham and cheese slices into the pockets. Mix a little seasoning with the flour and dust the chicken breasts with this. Coat with beaten egg and crumbs and fry steadily in oil or fat for about 12 to 15 minutes or until crisp, golden-brown and tender.
Serves 4.

Fish and bacon whirls

Finishing with Flair

CONTINENTAL CHOCOLATE SQUARES

IMPERIAL/METRIC	AMERICAN
Base	Base
4 oz. (100 grms.) butter or margarine	*½ cup butter or margarine*
4 oz. (100 grms.) sugar	*½ cup sugar*
1 tablespoon cocoa	*1 tablespoon cocoa*
1 egg	*1 egg*
½ teaspoon vanilla essence	*½ teaspoon vanilla extract*
8 oz. wholemeal biscuits, crushed	*2 cups crushed graham crackers*
4 oz. (100 grms.) desiccated coconut	*1 cup shredded coconut*
3 oz. (75 grms.) walnuts, chopped	*½ cup chopped walnuts*
Topping	Topping
4 oz. (100 grms.) butter or margarine	*½ cup butter or margarine*
1½ lb. (600 grms.) icing sugar	*4 cups confectioners' sugar*
2 tablespoons custard powder	*2 tablespoons custard powder*
2 tablespoons hot water	*2 tablespoons hot water*
1 tablespoon liqueur, rum or brandy	*1 tablespoon liqueur, rum or brandy*
6 oz. (150 grms.) plain chocolate	*6 oz. (6 squares) plain chocolate*

METHOD

To make the base, melt the butter or margarine and stir in the sugar and cocoa. Remove from the heat and mix in the egg, vanilla, biscuit (cracker) crumbs, coconut and walnuts. Spread on a greased baking sheet about 7×9 inches (17½×22½ cm.). Chill until set.

For the topping, melt the butter or margarine and stir in the sugar, custard powder, water and liqueur. Beat well until smooth and creamy. Spread over the base and chill until set. Melt the chocolate gently and spread it over the top. Chill until set. Twenty to 30 minutes before serving, allow the mixture to return to room temperature. Cut into 1 inch (2½ cm.) squares with a damp knife.

Makes about 50.

STRAWBERRIES IN GRAND MARNIER

IMPERIAL/METRIC	AMERICAN
2 lb. (1 kilo) strawberries	*2 lb. strawberries*
icing sugar	*confectioners' sugar*
6 tablespoons Grand Marnier	*6 tablespoons Grand Marnier*

METHOD

Put the strawberries in six individual glass serving dishes. Sprinkle with the sugar and Grand Marnier and leave to stand at room temperature for at least 1 hour.

Serves 6.

Continental chocolate squares

FRENCH CHERRY FRITTERS

IMPERIAL/METRIC

Sauce

1 lb. (½ kilo) black or Morello cherries

¼ pint (125 ml.) water

2 to 4 oz. (50 to 100 grms.) sugar

1 teaspoon arrowroot

3 to 4 tablespoons cherry brandy

Choux pastry

¼ pint (125 ml.) water

1 oz. (25 grms.) butter or margarine

3 oz. (75 grms.) flour

pinch of sugar

2 eggs plus 1 egg yolk

deep fat for frying

AMERICAN

Sauce

1 lb. black or Morello cherries

⅝ cup water

¼ to ½ cup sugar

1 teaspoon arrowroot

3 to 4 tablespoons cherry brandy

Choux pastry

⅝ cup water

2 tablespoons butter or margarine

¾ cup flour

pinch of sugar

2 eggs plus 1 egg yolk

deep fat for frying

METHOD

Put the cherries, water and sugar into a saucepan and simmer for 5 minutes. Blend the arrowroot with the cherry brandy and stir into the cherry mixture. Boil steadily until thickened. Keep hot.

Put the water and butter or margarine into a saucepan and heat until the butter or margarine has melted. Remove the pan from the heat and add the flour all at once with the sugar. Stir until the mixture forms a ball. Gradually add the eggs and egg yolk. Heat the oil to about 365°F or until a cube of stale bread dropped into the oil turns brown in just over 30 seconds. Either pipe or spoon the mixture into the fat and fry for 6 to 8 minutes or until golden-brown. Drain and keep hot. Pile the fritters in a pyramid and serve with the hot cherry sauce.

Serves 6 to 8.

French cherry fritters

GLAZED APPLES

IMPERIAL/METRIC

½ pint (250 ml.) water

juice of 1 lemon

strip of lemon rind

4 oz. (100 grms.) sugar

4 medium-sized cooking apples

1 tablespoon Curaçao

1 oz. (25 grms.) butter or margarine

AMERICAN

1¼ cups water

juice of 1 lemon

strip of lemon rind

½ cup sugar

4 medium-sized cooking apples

1 tablespoon Curaçao

2 tablespoons butter or margarine

METHOD

Put the water, lemon juice, lemon rind and sugar in a shallow saucepan. Stir to dissolve the sugar and bring to the boil. Peel the apples and place them in the pan. Poach gently until tender.

Add the Curaçao and butter or margarine and stir well. Turn the apples over in the syrup to coat them well.

Serves 4.

Mango mousse

MANGO MOUSSE

IMPERIAL/METRIC

1 lb. (½ kilo) fresh mango pulp or canned mangoes, drained
sugar
½ pint (250 ml.) double cream, whipped
1 tablespoon gelatine
3 tablespoons orange or lemon juice, warmed

AMERICAN

1 lb. fresh mango pulp or canned mangoes, drained
sugar
1¼ cups heavy cream, whipped
1 tablespoon gelatine
3 tablespoons orange or lemon juice, warmed

METHOD

Mix the mango pulp to a purée in a liquidiser or press through a sieve. Make the purée up to ½ pint (250 ml.)/ 1¼ cups with mango juice or water. Add sugar to taste. Mix in the whipped cream. Dissolve the gelatine in the orange or lemon juice and cool. Stir into the mango mixture. Pour into a serving dish and chill until set. **Serves 6.**

G is for . . . GOOD HEALTH: *choose the foods that help you look your best and feel great, because 'you are what you eat' . . .*
GOURMET'S TOUCH: *a little bit extra that can turn an ordinary meal into something much more special*

Good Health

BURGHUL SALAD

IMPERIAL/METRIC

8 oz. (200 grms.) fine burghul (cracked wheat) or kibble
3 tablespoons finely chopped spring onions or shallots
salt and pepper
$\frac{3}{4}$ pint (375 ml.) finely chopped parsley
15 to 20 tablespoons chopped fresh mint
2 tablespoons olive oil
2 tablespoons lemon juice

AMERICAN

2 cups fine burghul (cracked wheat) or kibble
3 tablespoons finely chopped scallions or shallots
salt and pepper
2 cups finely chopped parsley
15 to 20 tablespoons chopped fresh mint
2 tablespoons olive oil
2 tablespoons lemon juice

METHOD

Soak the burghul or kibble in water for about 30 minutes. It will expand enormously. Drain and wrap in a towel and squeeze out as much moisture as possible. Spread out to dry further. Mix the burghul or kibble with the spring onions (scallions) or shallots, crushing the onions as much as possible so that their juices run out. Season with salt and pepper and add the parsley, mint, olive oil and lemon juice. Mix well. Garnish with cucumber and black olives.
Serves 8.

Burghul salad

Garden cocktail

GARDEN COCKTAIL

IMPERIAL/METRIC	AMERICAN
8 oz. (200 grms.) carrots, chopped	*8 oz. carrots, chopped*
2 large apples, peeled, cored and chopped	*2 large apples, peeled, cored and chopped*
3 celery stalks, sliced	*3 celery stalks, sliced*
pepper	*pepper*
chopped walnuts	*chopped walnuts*

METHOD

Put the carrots, apples and celery in a liquidiser and blend until smooth. Season with pepper. Pour into glasses and garnish with the walnuts. You need a powerful liquidiser for this, so a juice extractor may be needed if the carrots are very crisp. Alternatively, you may use canned carrot juice.

Serves 3 to 4.

CHEESE AND DATE BREAD

IMPERIAL/METRIC	AMERICAN
8 oz. (200 grms.) self-raising flour	*2 cups self-rising flour*
1 teaspoon dry mustard	*1 teaspoon dry mustard*
salt and pepper	*salt and pepper*
2 oz. (50 grms.) butter or margarine	*$\frac{1}{4}$ cup butter or margarine*
4 oz. (100 grms.) Cheddar, Gruyère or Cheshire cheese, grated	*1 cup grated Cheddar, Gruyère or Cheshire cheese*
3 oz. (75 grms.) dates, chopped	*$\frac{1}{2}$ cup chopped dates*
2 eggs, beaten	*2 eggs, beaten*
$\frac{1}{4}$ pint (125 ml.) milk or buttermilk	*$\frac{5}{8}$ cup milk or buttermilk*

METHOD

Sift the flour, mustard and seasoning into a bowl. Rub in the butter or margarine, add the cheese and dates and mix well. Add one egg and nearly all of the second, reserving about 1 teaspoon to brush over the top of the loaf. Beat in the milk or buttermilk.

Put the dough into a greased and floured 1 pound ($\frac{1}{2}$ kilo) loaf tin and brush with the reserved egg. Bake in a moderate oven, 350°F, Gas Mark 4, for about 1 hour or until the loaf is firm to the touch. Reduce the heat after 30 minutes if the loaf is browning too much.

BANANA CREAM

IMPERIAL/METRIC	AMERICAN
2 large bananas	*2 large bananas*
4 tablespoons lemon juice	*4 tablespoons lemon juice*
4 tablespoons honey	*4 tablespoons honey*
$\frac{1}{2}$ pint (250 ml.) plain yogurt	*$1\frac{1}{4}$ cups plain yogurt*
4 tablespoons chopped nuts	*4 tablespoons chopped nuts*

METHOD

Mash the bananas with a fork and beat in the lemon juice and honey. Stir in the yogurt and most of the nuts. Spoon into four glasses and sprinkle with the remaining nuts.

Serves 4.

Gourmet's Touch

DRESSED CRAB

IMPERIAL/METRIC	AMERICAN
1 × 1 to 2 lb. (½ to 1 kilo) crab	*1 × 1 to 2 lb. crab*
salt and pepper	*salt and pepper*
¼ teaspoon dry mustard	*¼ teaspoon dry mustard*
1 hard-boiled egg	*1 hard-boiled egg*
lettuce leaves	*lettuce leaves*
lemon wedges	*lemon wedges*

METHOD

If the crab is alive, boil it gently in salted water for 15 minutes per pound. Cool in the liquid. When cold remove the big claws and twist off the small claws. Remove the undershell. Remove and discard the small sac from the top of the crab's shell, any green matter and the spongy fingers or lungs which lie around the big shell. Scrape the brown creamy part of the crab into a bowl. Remove the white flesh, separating it from the inner shell with a skewer or a pointed vegetable knife. Wash the shell well, using a small brush if necessary, and dry.

Crack the big claws, remove all the meat and shred it using a fork. Mix all the white meat together. Mix the brown creamy part with seasoning and mustard. Place the brown mixture across the centre of the shell with the white meat on either side. Garnish with chopped egg white and sieved egg yolk. Serve on a bed of lettuce leaves with lemon wedges.

Serves 1.

POTATOES DAUPHINE

IMPERIAL/METRIC	AMERICAN
8 oz. (200 grms) potatoes, cooked and mashed	*8 oz. potatoes, cooked and mashed*
salt and pepper	*salt and pepper*
Choux pastry	Choux pastry
2 oz. (50 grms.) butter or margarine	*¼ cup butter or margarine*
¼ pint (125 ml.) water	*⅝ cup water*
3 oz. (75 grms.) flour	*¾ cup flour*
2 eggs plus 1 egg yolk	*2 eggs plus 1 egg yolk*
salt and pepper	*salt and pepper*
deep fat for frying	*deep fat for frying*

METHOD

Beat the potatoes with seasoning until they are very smooth. Put the butter or margarine into a saucepan with the water and heat until the butter or margarine has melted. Remove the pan from the heat and add the flour all at once. Stir until the dough forms a ball. Gradually beat in the eggs and egg yolk and then blend in the potatoes. Taste for seasoning.

Dressed crab

Heat the fat for frying. To test if it is the right temperature, drop a cube of stale bread into it. The bread should turn golden-brown in just over 30 seconds. Either pipe or spoon the potato mixture into the fat and fry for a few minutes until golden brown. Drain.

Serves 4 to 6.

STUFFED PLAICE (FLOUNDER)

IMPERIAL/METRIC	AMERICAN
1 lb. (½ kilo) potatoes, cooked and mashed	*1 lb. potatoes, cooked and mashed*
salt and pepper	*salt and pepper*
2 oz. (50 grms.) butter or margarine	*¼ cup butter or margarine*
3 oz. (75 grms.) mushrooms, sliced	*3 oz. mushrooms, sliced*
3 to 4 lean bacon rashers, chopped	*3 to 4 lean bacon slices, chopped*
4 large or 8 small plaice fillets, skinned	*4 large or 8 small flounder fillets, skinned*
¼ pint (125 ml.) double cream	*⅝ cup heavy cream*
tomato	*tomato*
parsley sprigs	*parsley sprigs*

METHOD

Beat the potatoes with the seasoning and half the butter or margarine. Put into a cloth bag with a potato rose (large nozzle) and pipe a border around the edge of a shallow ovenproof dish. Fry the mushrooms and bacon in the remaining butter or margarine until just tender. Spoon this mixture into the centre of the fish fillets and roll them up, securing with wooden cocktail sticks. Put the fish rolls into the dish. Season the cream and pour it around the fish rolls. Cover the dish lightly with foil and bake in a moderate oven, 350°F, Gas Mark 4, for 15 minutes or until the fish is tender. Garnish with the tomato, cut decoratively, and parsley sprigs.
Serves 4.

Stuffed plaice (flounder)

SAVARIN

IMPERIAL/METRIC	AMERICAN
¼ oz. (6 grms.) fresh yeast	*¼ oz. fresh yeast*
1 teaspoon sugar	*1 teaspoon sugar*
6 fl. oz. (150 ml.) milk (hand-hot)	*¾ cup milk (hand-hot)*
6 oz. (150 grms.) flour	*1½ cups flour*
3 oz. (75 grms.) butter or margarine, melted	*⅜ cup butter or margarine, melted*
3 eggs, beaten	*3 eggs, beaten*
Syrup	Syrup
½ pint (250 ml.) water	*1¼ cups water*
4 oz. (100 grms.) sugar	*½ cup sugar*
juice of 1 to 2 lemons	*juice of 1 to 2 lemons*
2 to 3 tablespoons rum	*2 to 3 tablespoons rum*
Filling	Filling
fresh fruit	*fresh fruit*

METHOD

Cream the yeast with the sugar, add the milk and a sprinkling of the flour, and put in a warm place. Leave for 15 to 20 minutes or until the mixture is frothy. Sift in the rest of the flour and add the melted butter or margarine and eggs. Mix well. Pour into a well greased and warmed 9 to 10 inch (22½ to 25 cm.) ring cake tin that should be 3 to 4 inches (7½ to 10 cm.) deep. Cover lightly and leave in a warm place to rise for 45 minutes. Bake in a hot oven, 425°F, Gas Mark 7, for 25 to 30 minutes. After the first 15 minutes, reduce the oven temperature to fairly hot, 375°F, Gas Mark 5.

Meanwhile, heat the water, sugar and lemon juice until syrupy. Stir in the rum and keep the syrup hot.

Turn the cake out on to a wire cake rack, with a plate underneath. Prick with a fine skewer and pour over the hot syrup. When cool, lift on to a serving dish. Fill the centre of the ring with fresh fruit.
Serves 6 to 8.

Caramelized oranges

CARAMELIZED ORANGES

IMPERIAL/METRIC	AMERICAN
4 large oranges	*4 large oranges*
8 oz. (200 grms.) sugar	*1 cup sugar*
½ pint (250 ml.) water	*1¼ cups water*
1 tablespoon orange-flavoured liqueur	*1 tablespoon orange-flavored liqueur*

METHOD

Peel the oranges carefully, removing all white pith. Reserve the rind from two of the oranges and cut away all the white pith from it. Slice the rind into thin strips. Put the strips into a saucepan of cold water and bring to the boil. Boil for 10 minutes or until tender. Drain.

Dissolve the sugar in the water, then bring to the boil. Boil until thickish and syrupy. Stir in the liqueur. Add the oranges to the pan and turn over and over until they are well coated. Transfer the oranges to a serving dish. Add the strips of orange rind to the syrup and cook gently until they begin to look transparent and the syrup turns pale gold. Pile equal amounts of rind and syrup on each orange and chill.

Serves 4.

H *is for . . .* HERBS: *fresh or dried they enhance the natural flavours of the foods to which they are added . . .*
HOME BAKING: *set mouths watering with the aroma of freshly baked bread, scones and cakes that you have made yourself*

Herbs

Lamb shish-kebabs with herbed sauce

LAMB SHISH-KEBABS WITH HERBED SAUCE

IMPERIAL/METRIC	AMERICAN
1 lb. (½ kilo) lean lamb (from the leg), cut into 1 inch (2½ cm.) cubes	*1 lb. lean lamb (from the leg), cut into 1 inch cubes*
1 green pepper, pith and seeds removed, cut into chunks	*1 green pepper, pith and seeds removed, cut into cubes*
8 to 12 button mushrooms	*8 to 12 button mushrooms*
4 small tomatoes	*4 cherry tomatoes*
12 pickling onions	*12 baby onions*
1 oz. (25 grms.) butter or margarine, melted	*2 tablespoons butter or margarine, melted*
salt and pepper	*salt and pepper*
Sauce	Sauce
½ pint (250 ml.) tomato juice	*1¼ cups tomato juice*
2 teaspoons prepared mustard	*2 teaspoons prepared mustard*
¼ pint (125 ml.) plain yogurt	*⅝ cup plain yogurt*
pinch of cayenne pepper	*pinch of cayenne pepper*
2 teaspoons finely chopped fresh mint	*2 teaspoons finely chopped fresh mint*
2 teaspoons chopped chives or spring onions	*2 teaspoons chopped chives or scallions*
salt and pepper	*salt and pepper*
¼ teaspoon ground cinnamon	*¼ teaspoon ground cinnamon*

METHOD

Mix together all the ingredients for the sauce in a shallow dish. Put the lamb cubes into the sauce and leave to marinate for 3 to 4 hours, turning several times. Lift the meat out of the sauce and thread on to four skewers with the green pepper, mushrooms, tomatoes and onions. Brush the vegetables, not the meat, with the melted butter or margarine and season. Grill (broil), turning several times, until tender. Brush the meat once or twice with the sauce. Heat the remaining sauce gently and serve with the kebabs.

Serves 4.

HERB BUTTER

IMPERIAL/METRIC	AMERICAN
2 oz. (50 grms.) butter or margarine	*¼ cup butter or margarine*
1 teaspoon finely chopped fresh herbs	*1 teaspoon finely chopped fresh herbs*

METHOD

Blend the butter or margarine together with the herbs. Chill. You may use one herb or mix them. Serve on steaks, chops, sausages, grilled (broiled) fish, or jacket baked potatoes.

Herb butter

Scones

WHOLEMEAL BREAD

IMPERIAL/METRIC	AMERICAN
1 tablespoon sugar	*1 tablespoon sugar*
12 fl. oz. (300 ml.) water (hand-hot)	*$\frac{3}{4}$ pint water (hand-hot)*
1 tablespoon dried yeast	*1 tablespoon dried yeast*
1 tablespoon butter or margarine	*1 tablespoon butter or margarine*
$\frac{1}{2}$ teaspoon salt	*$\frac{1}{2}$ teaspoon salt*
1 lb. (400 grms.) medium or coarse stoneground wholemeal flour	*1 lb. medium or coarse stoneground wholemeal flour*

METHOD

Dissolve $\frac{1}{2}$ teaspoon of the sugar in one-third of the water. Sprinkle over the yeast and whisk in with a fork. Leave in a warm place for 10 to 15 minutes or until the mixture is frothy.

Dissolve the remaining sugar in the remaining water together with the butter or margarine and salt. Add to the flour with the yeast mixture and mix until a smooth dough is formed. Leave the dough in a warm place for about 30 minutes. Knead lightly and shape into a loaf. Put the loaf into a loaf tin and leave for a further 30 minutes in a warm place. Bake in a hot oven, 425°F, Gas Mark 7, for 35 to 40 minutes. The bread is done if it sounds hollow when knocked on the bottom with your knuckles.

Makes 1 loaf.

SCONES

IMPERIAL/METRIC	AMERICAN
8 oz. (200 grms.) flour	*2 cups flour*
$\frac{1}{2}$ teaspoon salt	*$\frac{1}{2}$ teaspoon salt*
1 teaspoon bicarbonate of soda	*1 teaspoon baking soda*
2 teaspoons cream of tartar	*2 teaspoons cream of tartar*
$1\frac{1}{2}$ oz. (38 grms.) butter or margarine	*3 tablespoons butter or margarine*
about $\frac{1}{4}$ pint (125 ml.) milk	*about $\frac{5}{8}$ cup milk*

METHOD

Sift the flour, salt, soda and cream of tartar into a bowl. Cut the butter or margarine into pieces and rub into the flour. Bind the mixture with enough milk to give a soft but not wet dough. Pat or roll out the dough on a lightly floured surface to $\frac{1}{2}$ inch ($1\frac{1}{4}$ cm.) thickness. Cut into circles and place on a baking sheet. Bake in a hot oven, 425°F, Gas Mark 7, for 10 minutes or until risen and golden brown.

Makes about 12.

Wholemeal bread

Brioches

BRIOCHES

IMPERIAL/METRIC	AMERICAN
1 tablespoon plus ½ teaspoon sugar	*1 tablespoon plus ½ teaspoon sugar*
3 tablespoons water (hand-hot)	*3 tablespoons water (hand-hot)*
2 teaspoons dried yeast	*2 teaspoons dried yeast*
8 oz. (200 grms.) flour	*2 cups flour*
½ teaspoon salt	*½ teaspoon salt*
2 eggs, beaten	*2 eggs, beaten*
2 oz. (50 grms.) butter or margarine, melted and cooled	*¼ cup butter or margarine, melted and cooled*
Egg glaze	Egg glaze
1 egg	*1 egg*
1 tablespoon water	*1 tablespoon water*
pinch of sugar	*pinch of sugar*

METHOD

Dissolve ½ teaspoon of the sugar in the water. Sprinkle over the yeast and whisk it in with a fork. Leave in a warm place for 10 to 15 minutes or until the mixture is frothy.

Sift the flour and salt into a bowl. Mix in the rest of the sugar, the yeast mixture, eggs and butter or margarine. Beat by hand until the mixture leaves the sides of the bowl. Knead on a lightly floured board for 5 minutes. Put the dough in a warm place and leave to rise for about 1½ hours, or until it has doubled in size and springs back when lightly pressed.

Divide the dough into 12 portions. Break off a small bit of each portion and roll into 12 small balls. Roll the remainder of the portions into 12 large balls. Make a hole in each large ball with a finger and place the small balls in these. Place the balls in tins and leave in a warm place to rise for about 1 hour, or until light and puffy. Mix together all the ingredients for the egg glaze and brush the brioches with the glaze. Bake in a very hot oven, 450°F, Gas Mark 8, for 10 minutes.

Makes 12.

ECONOMICAL DUNDEE CAKE

IMPERIAL/METRIC	AMERICAN
5 oz. (125 grms.) butter or margarine	*⅝ cup butter or margarine*
5 oz. (125 grms.) sugar	*⅝ cup sugar*
2 large eggs	*2 large eggs*
8 oz. (200 grms.) self-raising flour	*2 cups self-rising flour*
12 oz. (300 grms.) mixed dried fruit	*2 cups mixed dried fruit*
2 oz. (50 grms.) glacé cherries	*⅓ cup glacé cherries*
2 oz. (50 grms.) chopped candied peel	*⅓ cup chopped candied peel*
little milk	*little milk*
1 to 2 oz. (25 to 50 grms.) blanched almonds	*2 to 4 tablespoons blanched almonds*

METHOD

Cream the butter or margarine and sugar together. Gradually beat in the eggs. Sift in the flour and fold it in. Mix in the fruit, cherries and peel with enough milk to give a soft dropping consistency. Put into a greased and floured or lined and greased tin and cover with the almonds. Brush these with a little egg white – there is enough left in the egg shells after making the cake. Bake in a very moderate oven, 325°F, Gas Mark 3, for about 1¾ hours. Reduce the heat slightly after 45 minutes to 1 hour if the cake becomes too brown.

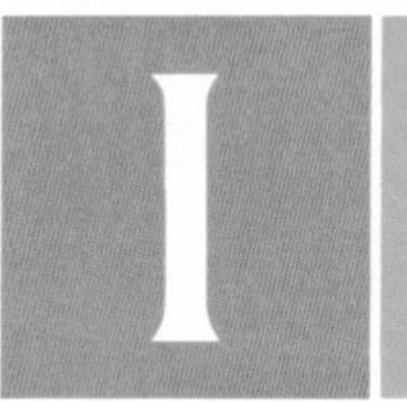

I *is for . . .* INSTANT MEALS: *cook these main dishes in a hurry and serve them with simple and quick-to-prepare accompaniments . . .* INFORMAL SUPPERS: *what to serve when good friends gather to enjoy a simple and convivial meal*

Instant Meals

CHEESE KEBABS

IMPERIAL/METRIC	AMERICAN
Edam or Gouda cheese, cut into cubes	*Edam or Gouda cheese, cut into cubes*
banana slices, brushed with lemon juice	*banana slices, brushed with lemon juice*
apple slices, brushed with lemon juice	*apple slices, brushed with lemon juice*
orange segments	*orange segments*
bacon rashers, rolled	*bacon slices, rolled*
button mushrooms	*button mushrooms*
baby tomatoes	*cherry tomatoes*
pieces of green pepper	*pieces of green pepper*
pickling onions	*baby onions*
melted butter or margarine	*melted butter or margarine*

METHOD

Thread the cheese, fruit, bacon and vegetables on to skewers. Brush with melted butter or margarine and cook for a few minutes under a hot grill (broiler).

VEAL ESCALOPES WITH LEMON

IMPERIAL/METRIC	AMERICAN
4 veal escalopes	*4 veal escalopes*
2 tablespoons flour	*2 tablespoons flour*
salt and pepper	*salt and pepper*
1 oz. (25 grms.) butter or margarine	*2 tablespoons butter or margarine*
1 tablespoon oil	*1 tablespoon oil*
juice of 1 lemon	*juice of 1 lemon*
2 tablespoons sherry	*2 tablespoons sherry*
1 teaspoon sugar	*1 teaspoon sugar*
$\frac{1}{4}$ pint (125 ml.) single cream	*$\frac{5}{8}$ cup light cream*

METHOD

Coat the veal with the flour seasoned with salt and pepper. Fry in the butter or margarine and oil for about 8 minutes, turning once. Transfer the escalopes to a hot serving dish. Add the lemon juice, sherry and sugar to the juices in the pan and heat for 2 minutes, stirring. Stir in the cream and heat gently. Do not allow to boil. Spoon the sauce over the veal.

Serves 4.

Cheese kebabs

VEGETABLE RISOTTO

IMPERIAL/METRIC	AMERICAN
2 large onions, sliced	*2 large onions, sliced*
1 garlic clove, crushed	*1 garlic clove, crushed*
2 tablespoons oil	*2 tablespoons oil*
1 lb. ($\frac{1}{2}$ kilo) tomatoes, skinned and sliced	*1 lb. tomatoes, skinned and sliced*
6 oz. (150 grms.) long-grain rice	*1 cup long-grain rice*
1 pint ($\frac{1}{2}$ l.) water	*$2\frac{1}{2}$ cups water*
2 large carrots, diced or grated	*2 large carrots, diced or grated*
few peas (fresh or frozen)	*few peas (fresh or frozen)*
salt and pepper	*salt and pepper*
4 oz. (100 grms.) mushrooms, sliced	*4 oz. mushrooms, sliced*
2 tablespoons chopped parsley	*2 tablespoons chopped parsley*
8 oz. (200 grms.) Cheddar or Gruyère cheese, grated	*2 cups grated Cheddar or Gruyère cheese*

METHOD

Fry the onions and garlic in the oil for a few minutes, then remove some of the onion rings. Stir some of the tomato slices and the rice into the onions in the pan. Add the water and bring to the boil. Stir in the carrots and peas and cook for about 10 minutes. Season well. Add the remaining tomato slices, the mushrooms and the reserved onion rings. Cook gently until the rice is tender and most of the liquid has been absorbed.

Mix in half the parsley and half the cheese. Pile the risotto on to a hot serving dish and top with the rest of the parsley and cheese.

Serves 4 to 6.

Vegetable risotto

LEMON GARLIC KIDNEYS

IMPERIAL/METRIC	AMERICAN
12 lambs' kidneys, skinned, cored and halved	*12 lambs' kidneys, skinned, cored and halved*
salt and pepper	*salt and pepper*
1 garlic clove, crushed	*1 garlic clove, crushed*
2 tablespoons olive oil	*2 tablespoons olive oil*
juice of 1 lemon	*juice of 1 lemon*
hot boiled rice	*hot boiled rice*

METHOD

Season the kidneys and fry them with the garlic in the oil for 3 to 4 minutes, stirring frequently. Squeeze the lemon juice into the pan and toss well. Serve on a bed of rice.

Serves 4.

Informal Suppers

CHEESE FONDUE

IMPERIAL/METRIC	AMERICAN
1 garlic clove, halved	*1 garlic clove, halved*
$\frac{1}{2}$ pint (250 ml.) dry white wine	*$1\frac{1}{4}$ cups dry white wine*
1 lb. ($\frac{1}{2}$ kilo) Gruyère cheese, grated	*1 lb. Gruyère cheese, grated*
1 teaspoon arrowroot	*1 teaspoon arrowroot*
2 tablespoons kirsch	*2 tablespoons kirsch*
$\frac{1}{2}$ oz. ($12\frac{1}{2}$ grms.) butter or margarine	*1 tablespoon butter or margarine*
French bread, cut into cubes	*French bread, cut into cubes*

METHOD

Rub the inside of the fondue pot with the garlic, then discard it. Add the wine, heat for a minute and then add the cheese. Stir constantly in a figure eight motion until the cheese melts and the fondue thickens. Mix the arrowroot with the kirsch and stir into the cheese mixture. Add the butter or margarine and stir until it has melted. Serve with the bread cubes for dipping.
Serves 3 to 4.

SPAGHETTI ETCETERA

IMPERIAL/METRIC	AMERICAN
8 oz. (200 grms.) spaghetti	*8 oz. spaghetti*
8 oz. (200 grms.) mushrooms, sliced	*8 oz. mushrooms, sliced*
2 onions, thinly sliced	*2 onions, thinly sliced*
2 garlic cloves, crushed	*2 garlic cloves, crushed*
12 anchovy fillets, chopped	*12 anchovy fillets, chopped*
6 bacon rashers, chopped	*6 bacon slices, chopped*
12 black olives, stoned	*12 black olives, stoned*
4 tablespoons chopped parsley	*4 tablespoons chopped parsley*
3 tablespoons olive oil	*3 tablespoons olive oil*
grated Parmesan cheese	*grated Parmesan cheese*

METHOD

Cook the spaghetti in boiling salted water for about 15 to 20 minutes or until tender. Meanwhile, gently cook the mushrooms, onions, garlic, anchovy fillets, bacon, olives and parsley in the oil, covered, for about 15 minutes. When the spaghetti is cooked, drain it well and put on a hot serving dish. Top with the mushroom mixture and serve with Parmesan cheese.

Serves 4.

Cheese fondue

Pizza neapolitan

PIZZA NEAPOLITAN

IMPERIAL/METRIC	AMERICAN
Dough	Dough
$\frac{1}{4}$ teaspoon sugar	*$\frac{1}{4}$ teaspoon sugar*
$\frac{1}{4}$ pint (125 ml.) water (hand-hot)	*$\frac{5}{8}$ cup water (hand-hot)*
1 teaspoon dried yeast	*1 teaspoon dried yeast*
8 oz. (200 grms.) flour	*2 cups flour*
1 teaspoon salt	*1 teaspoon salt*
$\frac{1}{2}$ oz. (12$\frac{1}{2}$ grms.) butter or margarine	*1 tablespoon butter or margarine*
Filling	Filling
olive oil	*olive oil*
6 tomatoes, skinned and sliced	*6 tomatoes, skinned and sliced*
1 garlic clove, finely chopped	*1 garlic clove, finely chopped*
12 anchovy fillets	*12 anchovy fillets*
4 oz. (100 grms.) Mozzarella cheese, thinly sliced	*4 oz. Mozzarella cheese, thinly sliced*
black olives, stoned	*black olives, stoned*
dried oregano	*dried oregano*
black pepper	*black pepper*

METHOD

To make the dough, dissolve the sugar in the warm water and sprinkle the yeast on top. Leave in a warm place for 10 to 15 minutes or until frothy. Meanwhile, sift the flour and salt into a bowl and rub in the butter or margarine. Mix to a soft dough with the yeast mixture, adding a little extra flour if the dough is too sticky. Knead for 10 minutes or until the dough is smooth and elastic, then put into an oiled bowl. Cover with oiled paper and leave to rise in a warm place until the dough doubles in size.

Turn out on to a floured surface and knead lightly. Roll out into a $\frac{1}{4}$ inch ($\frac{3}{4}$ cm.) thick circle and transfer it to an oiled baking sheet. Brush with olive oil, then cover with slices of tomato sprinkled with garlic. Top with anchovy fillets, slices of cheese and olives. Sprinkle with oregano and pepper and bake in a hot oven, 450°F, Gas Mark 8, for 25 to 30 minutes.

Serves 2.

DEVILLED POTATO SALAD WITH FRANKFURTERS

IMPERIAL/METRIC	AMERICAN
1 lb. (400 grms.) potatoes	*1 lb. potatoes*
5 tablespoons olive oil	*5 tablespoons olive oil*
2 tablespoons vinegar	*2 tablespoons vinegar*
salt and pepper	*salt and pepper*
1 garlic clove, crushed	*1 garlic clove, crushed*
2 teaspoons French mustard	*2 teaspoons French mustard*
dash of Worcestershire sauce	*dash of Worcestershire sauce*
pinch of cayenne pepper	*pinch of cayenne pepper*
3 tomatoes, skinned and chopped	*3 tomatoes, skinned and chopped*
$\frac{1}{2}$ green pepper, pith and seeds removed and chopped	*$\frac{1}{2}$ green pepper, pith and seeds removed and chopped*
6 spring onions, chopped	*6 scallions, chopped*
paprika	*paprika*
8 frankfurters, split, cooked and kept warm	*8 frankfurters, split, cooked and kept warm*

METHOD

Cook the potatoes in boiling salted water until they are tender. Meanwhile, mix together the oil, vinegar, seasoning, garlic, mustard, Worcestershire sauce and cayenne pepper. When the potatoes are cooked, drain and cut into bite-sized pieces. Mix with the dressing while still warm. Mix in the tomatoes, green pepper and spring onions (scallions). Pile on to a dish and sprinkle with paprika. Arrange the frankfurters around the edge and serve warm or cold.

Serves 4.

SOMERSET PORK

IMPERIAL/METRIC	AMERICAN
1 to $1\frac{1}{4}$ lb. ($\frac{1}{2}$ kilo) pork fillet	*1 to $1\frac{1}{4}$ lb. pork fillet*
2 tablespoons flour	*2 tablespoons flour*
2 oz. (50 grms.) butter or margarine	*$\frac{1}{4}$ cup butter or margarine*
1 large onion, finely chopped	*1 large onion, finely chopped*
6 oz. (150 grms.) mushrooms, sliced	*6 oz. mushrooms, sliced*
$\frac{1}{2}$ pint (250 ml.) cider	*$1\frac{1}{4}$ cups cider*
salt and pepper	*salt and pepper*
4 tablespoons double cream	*4 tablespoons heavy cream*
chopped parsley	*chopped parsley*

METHOD

Cut the pork fillet into eight pieces. Place each piece between two sheets of greaseproof (waxed) paper and beat with a meat hammer or rolling pin until it is $\frac{1}{4}$ inch ($\frac{3}{4}$ cm.) thick. Coat the pork lightly with the flour and fry slowly in the butter or margarine for about 4 minutes on each side. Remove from the pan and keep warm.

Add the onion and mushrooms to the pan and cook until tender. Stir in any remaining flour. Gradually add the cider, stirring constantly. Bring to the boil, stirring. Return the pork to the pan and season well. Stir in the cream and heat gently. Do not allow to boil. Garnish with parsley.

Serves 4.

KIDNEY KEBABS WITH BARBECUE SAUCE

IMPERIAL/METRIC	AMERICAN
8 pickling onions	*8 baby onions*
4 bacon rashers, cut in half and rolled up	*4 bacon slices, cut in half and rolled up*
4 lambs' kidneys, skinned, cored and halved	*4 lambs' kidneys, skinned, cored and halved*
4 chipolata sausages, halved	*4 chipolata sausages, halved*
1 teaspoon tomato purée	*1 teaspoon tomato purée*
1 teaspoon Worcestershire sauce	*1 teaspoon Worcestershire sauce*
1 tablespoon oil	*1 tablespoon oil*
hot boiled rice	*hot boiled rice*
Sauce	Sauce
1 onion, finely chopped	*1 onion, finely chopped*
$\frac{1}{2}$ oz. ($12\frac{1}{2}$ grms.) butter or margarine	*1 tablespoon butter or margarine*
$\frac{1}{4}$ pint (125 ml.) tomato ketchup	*$\frac{5}{8}$ cup tomato ketchup*
2 tablespoons honey	*2 tablespoons honey*
2 tablespoons lemon juice	*2 tablespoons lemon juice*
salt and pepper	*salt and pepper*

Kidney kebabs with barbecue sauce

METHOD

Cook the onions in boiling salted water for 4 minutes and drain. Thread the onions, bacon rolls, kidneys and sausages on to skewers. Mix together the tomato purée, Worcestershire sauce and oil. Brush this all over the kebabs and cook under the grill (broiler) for about 10 minutes. Turn once and baste with the oil mixture.

To make the sauce, fry the onion in the butter or margarine until soft. Add the remaining ingredients and bring to the boil. Simmer for 5 minutes.

Serve the kebabs on the rice with the sauce.

Serves 4.

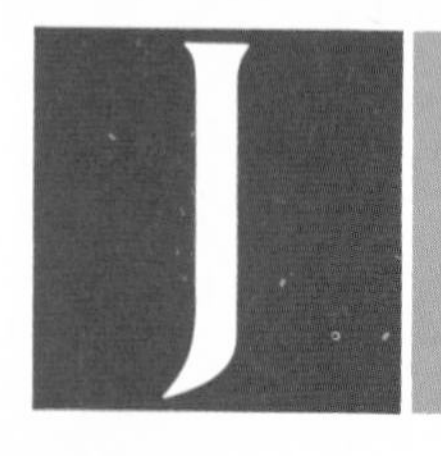

J is for . . . JAMS: *nothing is nicer than homemade, and you can make good use of the fruits in season . . .* JUST FOR TWO: *if there are only two of you, or if there is a special man you want to impress, here are some suggestions*

Jam

PEAR AND APRICOT JAM

IMPERIAL/METRIC	AMERICAN
1 lb. (½ kilo) pears, peeled, cored and sliced	*1 lb. pears, peeled, cored and sliced*
1 lb. (½ kilo) apricots, halved and stoned	*1 lb. apricots, halved and stoned*
½ pint (250 ml.) water	*1¼ cups water*
4 lemons	*4 lemons*
4 lb. (2 kilos) sugar	*4 lb. sugar*

Jams

METHOD

Put the pears, apricots and water in a preserving pan. Cut the lemons in half and squeeze the juice into the pan. Slice the skins and tie them loosely in a muslin (cheesecloth) bag. Put it in the pan. Bring to the boil, reduce the heat and simmer until the fruit is tender. Remove the muslin (cheesecloth) bag, squeezing out the juice. Add the sugar and stir until dissolved. Boil rapidly until setting point is reached. Skim and pour into hot clean jars. Cover.

Makes about 7 pounds (3¼ kilograms).

GREENGAGE JAM

IMPERIAL/METRIC	AMERICAN
3 lb. (1½ kilos) greengages, halved and stones removed	*3 lb. greengages, halved and stones removed*
¼ to ¾ pint (125 to 375 ml.) water	*⅝ to 2 cups water*
3 lb. (1½ kilos) sugar	*3 lb. sugar*

METHOD

Place the greengages in a preserving pan with ¼ pint or 125 ml. (⅝ cup) water. Crack some of the stones, remove the kernels and blanch them in boiling water for 1 minute. Remove the skins, split the kernels in half and add them to the greengages. Bring to the boil and simmer until the greengages are tender. Add extra water if necessary. Add the sugar and stir until dissolved. Boil rapidly until setting point is reached. Skim and pour into hot clean jars. Cover.

Makes about 5 pounds (2¼ kilograms).

APPLE AND GINGER JAM

IMPERIAL/METRIC	AMERICAN
3 lb. (1½ kilos) apples, peeled, cored and chopped	*3 lb. apples, peeled, cored and chopped*
1 pint (½ l.) water	*2½ cups water*
juice and thinly pared rind of 2 lemons	*juice and thinly pared rind of 2 lemons*
2 tablespoons ground ginger or 2 oz. (50 grms.) root ginger, bruised	*2 tablespoons ground ginger or 2 medium-sized fresh ginger root, bruised*
3 lb. (1½ kilos) sugar	*3 lb. sugar*

METHOD

Put the apples, water, lemon juice and ground ginger (if used) in a preserving pan. Tie the apple peel and cores, lemon rind and root ginger (if used) in a muslin (cheesecloth) bag and add to the pan. Bring to the boil, reduce the heat and simmer until the apple is tender. Remove the muslin (cheesecloth) bag and squeeze out the juice. Add the sugar and stir until dissolved. Boil rapidly until setting point is reached. Skim and pour into hot clean jars. Cover.

Makes about 5 pounds (2¼ kilograms).

Just for Two

Pepper steaks

GAMMON (HAM) WITH PINEAPPLE AND CORN SAUCE

IMPERIAL/METRIC	AMERICAN
2 slices of lean gammon	*2 slices of lean smoked ham*
2 oz. (50 grms.) butter or margarine, melted	*$\frac{1}{4}$ cup butter or margarine, melted*
3 to 4 canned pineapple rings, halved	*3 to 4 canned pineapple rings, halved*
Sauce	Sauce
$\frac{1}{2}$ oz. ($12\frac{1}{2}$ grms.) butter or margarine	*1 tablespoon butter or margarine*
$\frac{1}{2}$ oz. ($12\frac{1}{2}$ grms.) flour	*2 tablespoons flour*
$\frac{1}{4}$ pint (125 ml.) milk	*$\frac{5}{8}$ cup milk*
salt and pepper	*salt and pepper*
1 small onion, chopped	*1 small onion, chopped*
4 tablespoons cooked sweetcorn	*4 tablespoons cooked corn*
2 teaspoons chopped parsley	*2 teaspoons chopped parsley*
watercress	*watercress*
2 tablespoons syrup from the can of pineapple	*2 tablespoons syrup from the can of pineapple*

METHOD

Snip the fat of the gammon (ham). Brush it with melted butter or margarine and grill (broil) for several minutes on one side. Turn, brush with more butter or margarine and continue cooking. When the gammon (ham) is nearly ready, add the pineapple rings to the grill (broiler) pan. Brush them with the remainder of the melted butter or margarine and heat thoroughly.

Meanwhile, melt the butter or margarine in a saucepan and stir in the flour. Cook, stirring, for 1 minute. Gradually add the milk, stirring constantly, and simmer until the mixture is thick. Add seasoning, the onion, sweetcorn and parsley and warm gently. Place the gammon (ham) and pineapple on a plate and garnish with watercress. At the last minute whisk the pineapple syrup into the sauce.

Serves 2.

PEPPER STEAKS

IMPERIAL/METRIC	AMERICAN
2 × 4 to 8 oz. (100 to 200 grms.) fillet or rump steaks	*2 × 4 to 8 oz. fillet or rump steaks*
1 tablespoon whole black peppercorns	*1 tablespoon whole black peppercorns*
2 oz. (50 grms.) butter or margarine	*$\frac{1}{4}$ cup butter or margarine*
1 tablespoon olive oil	*1 tablespoon olive oil*
2 teaspoons brandy	*2 teaspoons brandy*

METHOD

Trim the steaks neatly and beat them with a rolling pin. Crush the peppercorns coarsely with the rolling pin and press them into the steaks on both sides. Leave for about 1 hour. Fry the steaks quickly in the butter or margarine and oil to seal in the juices. Complete the cooking according to taste – rare, medium or well-done. Remove the steaks from the pan and keep hot.

Stir the brandy into the juices in the pan and bring to the boil, stirring. Pour this sauce over the steaks.

Serves 2.

Gammon (ham) with pineapple and corn sauce

TUNA FISH PROVENCALE

IMPERIAL/METRIC	AMERICAN
2 × 7 oz. (175 grms.) cans tuna	*2 × 7 oz. cans tuna*
juice of ½ lemon	*juice of ½ lemon*
salt and pepper	*salt and pepper*
4 anchovy fillets	*4 anchovy fillets*
1 onion, chopped	*1 onion, chopped*
1 tablespoon olive oil	*1 tablespoon olive oil*
4 tomatoes, skinned and chopped	*4 tomatoes, skinned and chopped*
1 garlic clove, crushed	*1 garlic clove, crushed*
1 bouquet garni	*1 bouquet garni*
¼ pint (125 ml.) white wine	*⅝ cup white wine*
chopped parsley	*chopped parsley*

METHOD

Remove the tuna from the cans very carefully so that they stay in shape and place side by side on an oven-proof dish. Sprinkle with lemon juice and season lightly. Arrange the anchovy fillets on top.

Fry the onion in the oil until soft. Add the tomatoes, garlic, bouquet garni and wine and bring to the boil. Boil rapidly until this sauce is reduced and thickened. Pour the sauce over the tuna, cover and bake in a moderate oven, 350°F, Gas Mark 4, for 15 minutes. Remove the bouquet garni. Sprinkle with parsley.

Serves 2.

Tuna fish provencale

SPINACH SALAD

IMPERIAL/METRIC	AMERICAN
8 oz. (200 grms.) fresh spinach	*8 oz. fresh spinach*
2 potatoes, cooked, cooled and thinly sliced	*2 potatoes, cooked, cooled and thinly sliced*
3 slices Gruyère cheese, cut into strips	*3 slices Gruyère cheese, cut into strips*
1 tablespoon double cream	*1 tablespoon heavy cream*
juice of ¼ lemon	*juice of ¼ lemon*
salt and pepper	*salt and pepper*

METHOD

Wash the spinach and put into a saucepan. There should be enough water left on the leaves so that you do not need to add any more. Cook for 3 minutes, covered, then drain well and squeeze out any excess water. Mix with the remaining ingredients and serve hot or cold.

Serves 2.

HAMBURGERS

IMPERIAL/METRIC	AMERICAN
2 small onions	*2 small onions*
8 oz. (200 grms.) lean minced beef	*8 oz. lean ground beef*
salt and pepper	*salt and pepper*
pinch of dried mixed herbs	*pinch of dried mixed herbs*
1 teaspoon chopped parsley	*1 teaspoon chopped parsley*
1 potato, peeled and grated	*1 potato, peeled and grated*
few drops Worcestershire sauce	*few drops Worcestershire sauce*
fat for frying	*fat for frying*
2 hamburger rolls or baps	*2 hamburger buns*
1 tomato, sliced	*1 tomato, sliced*

METHOD

Slice one onion and set aside. Grate the other and mix it with the beef, seasoning, herbs, potato and Worcestershire sauce. Divide the mixture in half and form into two patties. Fry the hamburgers in fat for about 4 minutes on one side, then turn over and add the sliced onion. Fry for a further 5 to 6 minutes. Put the hamburgers on the rolls (buns) and top with some sliced onion and a slice of tomato.

Serves 2.

Sesame chicken

SESAME CHICKEN

IMPERIAL/METRIC	AMERICAN
2 chicken breasts, boned	*2 chicken breasts, boned*
2 oz. (50 grms.) butter or margarine, melted	*¼ cup butter or margarine, melted*
1 tablespoon soya sauce	*1 tablespoon soy sauce*
1 tablespoon white wine	*1 tablespoon white wine*
pinch of dried tarragon	*pinch of dried tarragon*
½ teaspoon dry mustard	*½ teaspoon dry mustard*
sesame seeds	*sesame seeds*

METHOD

Put the chicken breasts in a shallow dish. Mix together the butter or margarine, soya sauce, wine, tarragon and mustard. Pour this mixture over the chicken and leave to marinate for 3 hours. Drain and reserve the marinade.

Grill (broil) the chicken for 4 to 6 minutes on each side. Remove from the heat, brush with the reserved marinade and roll in sesame seeds. Return to the heat and grill (broil) until the sesame seeds are golden brown.

Serves 2.

K is for . . . KITCHEN AIDS: *liquidizers, electric mixers, home freezers save you time and trouble and can make cooking more fun . . .* KNOW YOUR VEGETABLES: *make a change from traditional and straightforward vegetable dishes*

Kitchen Aids

SMOKED MACKEREL PATE

IMPERIAL/METRIC	AMERICAN
2 large smoked mackerel, skinned and boned	*2 large smoked mackerel, skinned and boned*
3 oz. (75 grms.) cream cheese	*3 oz. cream cheese*
juice of ½ lemon	*juice of ½ lemon*
10 oz. (250 grms.) butter or margarine, melted	*1¼ cups butter or margarine, melted*
salt and pepper	*salt and pepper*

METHOD

Purée the mackerel in a liquidizer or mash it well with a fork. Gradually add the remaining ingredients and blend until smooth. Turn into a terrine and chill.

Serves 6.

LASAGNE AL FORNO

IMPERIAL/METRIC	AMERICAN
Bolognese sauce	Bolognese sauce
2 streaky bacon rashers, chopped	*2 fatty bacon slices, chopped*
1 lb. (400 grms) lean minced beef	*1 lb. lean ground beef*
1 large onion, chopped	*1 large onion, chopped*
2 tablespoons oil	*2 tablespoons oil*
2 celery stalks, chopped	*2 celery stalks, chopped*
1 garlic clove, crushed	*1 garlic clove, crushed*
¼ teaspoon dried mixed herbs	*¼ teaspoon dried mixed herbs*
2 teaspoons salt	*2 teaspoons salt*
½ teaspoon sugar	*½ teaspoon sugar*
pinch of pepper	*pinch of pepper*
5 tablespoons tomato purée	*5 tablespoons tomato purée*
8 fl. oz. (200 ml.) water	*1 cup water*
Béchamel sauce	Béchamel sauce
¾ pint (375 ml.) milk	*2 cups milk*
1 bay leaf	*1 bay leaf*
2 peppercorns	*2 peppercorns*
1 mace blade	*1 mace blade*
few parsley sprigs	*few parsley sprigs*
small carrot, chopped	*small carrot, chopped*
piece of onion	*piece of onion*
1 oz. (25 grms.) butter or margarine	*2 tablespoons butter or margarine*
1 oz. (25 grms.) flour	*¼ cup flour*
salt and pepper	*salt and pepper*
Pasta	Pasta
2 teaspoons oil	*2 teaspoons oil*
2 teaspoons salt	*2 teaspoons salt*
4 oz. (100 grms.) lasagne	*4 oz. lasagne*
4 oz. (100 grms.) Gruyère cheese, grated	*1 cup grated Gruyère cheese*
2 oz. (50 grms.) Parmesan cheese, grated	*½ cup grated Parmesan cheese*

METHOD

Fry the bacon, beef and onion in the oil until brown, stirring frequently. Add all the remaining ingredients for the bolognese sauce and simmer, covered, for 1 hour.

To make the béchamel sauce, heat the milk with the herbs, peppercorns and vegetables, covered, for 10 minutes. Strain. Melt the butter and stir in the flour. Cook, stirring, for 1 minute. Gradually add the milk, stirring constantly, and simmer until the sauce has thickened. Add seasoning to taste and keep warm.

To cook the pasta, bring about 4 pints or 2 litres of water to the boil with the oil and salt. Add the lasagne and boil for 8 minutes. Drain. Assemble the lasagne al forno in layers in a 3 pint (1¾ litre) or 4 pint shallow ovenproof dish lined with aluminium foil. Start with a layer of bolognese sauce, then a layer of pasta, then a layer of béchamel sauce and Gruyère cheese. Continue making layers and end with the Parmesan cheese. Open freeze, then put in a polythene bag, seal, label and freeze. To thaw, bake in a fairly hot oven, 375°F, Gas Mark 5, for about 1 hour, or until the top is golden brown.

Serves 4 to 6.

Smoked mackerel pate

Know Your Vegetables

CAULIFLOWER SOUP

IMPERIAL/METRIC	AMERICAN
1 large onion, sliced	*1 large onion, sliced*
1 garlic clove, crushed	*1 garlic clove, crushed*
2 oz. (50 grms.) butter or margarine	*$\frac{1}{4}$ cup butter or margarine*
1 medium-sized cauliflower, broken into flowerets	*1 medium-sized cauliflower, broken into flowerets*
$1\frac{3}{4}$ pints (1 l.) chicken stock	*$2\frac{1}{4}$ pints chicken stock*
salt and pepper	*salt and pepper*
4 tablespoons single cream	*4 tablespoons light cream*
2 slices toast	*2 slices toast*
chopped parsley	*chopped parsley*

METHOD

Fry the onion and garlic slowly in the butter or margarine until soft. Add the cauliflower, stock and seasoning to taste and bring to the boil. Cover and simmer for 1 hour. Purée the soup in a liquidizer and return it to the pan. Stir in the cream and heat gently. Do not allow to boil. Cut the toast into $\frac{1}{2}$ inch ($1\frac{1}{4}$ cm.) cubes and scatter on top of the soup with the parsley.

Serves 4 to 6.

FRIED BEANS

IMPERIAL/METRIC	AMERICAN
1 onion, thinly sliced	*1 onion, thinly sliced*
1 garlic clove, crushed	*1 garlic clove, crushed*
1 tablespoon olive oil	*1 tablespoon olive oil*
1 lb. ($\frac{1}{2}$ kilo) green beans, coarsely chopped	*1 lb. green beans, coarsely chopped*
1 large tomato, skinned and chopped	*1 large tomato, skinned and chopped*
1 chilli pepper, seeds removed and finely chopped	*1 chilli pepper, seeds removed and finely chopped*
1 tablespoon sugar	*1 tablespoon sugar*
salt	*salt*
1 tablespoon coconut cream or 1 tablespoon desiccated coconut blended with 1 tablespoon hot cream	*1 tablespoon coconut cream or 1 tablespoon shredded coconut blended with 1 tablespoon hot cream*

METHOD

Fry the onion and garlic in the oil until soft. Add all the remaining ingredients except the coconut cream and stir until glazed. Cover and simmer gently for about 20 minutes or until the beans are tender. Add the coconut cream and stir until it has melted.

Serves 4.

Cauliflower soup

SWEET AND SOUR CABBAGE

IMPERIAL/METRIC	AMERICAN
1 red cabbage	*1 red cabbage*
2 cooking apples, peeled, cored and thinly sliced	*2 cooking apples, peeled, cored and thinly sliced*
2 onions, thinly sliced	*2 onions, thinly sliced*
salt and pepper	*salt and pepper*
2 tablespoons sugar	*2 tablespoons sugar*
1 parsley sprig	*1 parsley sprig*
1 bay leaf	*1 bay leaf*
½ teaspoon dried thyme	*½ teaspoon dried thyme*
2 tablespoons port wine	*2 tablespoons port wine*
2 tablespoons wine vinegar	*2 tablespoons wine vinegar*

METHOD

Shred the cabbage after removing the hard stalk. Put the cabbage into a casserole in alternating layers with the apples and onions. Season each layer with salt, pepper and sugar. Put the herbs in the middle layer. Pour the port and vinegar over and cook, covered, in a low oven, 300°F, Gas Mark 2, for 2 hours.

Serves 4.

SPINACH NICOISE

IMPERIAL/METRIC	AMERICAN
2 lb. (1 kilo) fresh spinach	*2 lb. fresh spinach*
3 oz. (75 grms.) butter or margarine	*⅜ cup butter or margarine*
2 tablespoons double cream	*2 tablespoons heavy cream*
salt and pepper	*salt and pepper*
2 onions, chopped	*2 onions, chopped*
4 large tomatoes, skinned and chopped	*4 large tomatoes, skinned and chopped*
4 oz. (100 grms.) Cheddar or Gruyère cheese, grated	*1 cup grated Cheddar or Gruyère cheese*

METHOD

Wash the spinach and put it in a saucepan. There should be enough water left on the leaves so that you do not need to add any more. Cook the spinach for 7 to 10 minutes or until it is just tender. Drain, pressing out all the excess water, and chop the spinach. Return to the pan with half the butter or margarine, the cream and seasoning to taste. Stir well and keep warm.

Fry the onions in the remaining butter or margarine until soft. Add the tomatoes and cook gently for 2 to 3 minutes. Add the cheese and seasoning to taste and remove from the heat.

Put the creamed spinach into a shallow hot flameproof dish and top with the hot tomato and cheese mixture. Heat for a few minutes under the grill (broiler) until the cheese has melted and the top is lightly brown.

Serves 4.

Sweet and sour cabbage

Stuffed tomatoes

STUFFED TOMATOES

IMPERIAL/METRIC	AMERICAN
6 large firm tomatoes	*6 large firm tomatoes*
1 lb. (½ kilo) spinach	*1 lb. spinach*
2 oz. (50 grms.) butter or margarine	*¼ cup butter or margarine*
1 to 2 garlic cloves, crushed	*1 to 2 garlic cloves, crushed*
2 to 3 tablespoons pine nuts	*2 to 3 tablespoons pine nuts*
salt and pepper	*salt and pepper*

METHOD

Cut the tops off the tomatoes and carefully scoop out the pulp. Put the tomatoes upside-down to drain.

Wash the spinach thoroughly and put into a saucepan. There should be enough water left on the leaves so that you do not need to add any more. Cook, covered, for 7 to 10 minutes or until just tender. Drain well, pressing out all excess moisture. Chop the spinach very finely or purée in a liquidiser or mouli food mill. Mix in half the butter or margarine and the garlic.

Fry the pine nuts in the remaining butter or margarine until they are crisp and golden. Drain and add to the spinach purée with seasoning. Mix well and spoon into the tomato cases. Bake in a moderate oven, 350°F, Gas Mark 4, for 20 to 30 minutes or until heated through. The tomatoes should not become soft.

Serves 6.

LYONNAISE POTATOES

IMPERIAL/METRIC	AMERICAN
1 lb. (400 grms.) potatoes, peeled and thinly sliced	*1 lb. potatoes, peeled and thinly sliced*
1 large onion, thinly sliced	*1 large onion, thinly sliced*
2 oz. (50 grms.) butter or margarine	*¼ cup butter or margarine*
salt and pepper	*salt and pepper*
chopped parsley	*chopped parsley*

METHOD

Blanch the potato slices in boiling water for 1 minute, then drain. Fry the onion in the butter or margarine until soft. Layer the onion, potatoes and seasoning in a greased 2 pint (1 litre) 5 cup casserole, finishing with a layer of potatoes. Pour over any butter or margarine left in the pan, cover and bake in a moderately hot oven, 400°F, Gas Mark 6, for 1½ hours. Remove the lid for the last 30 minutes so that the potatoes can brown. Sprinkle with parsley.

Serves 4.

Lyonnaise potatoes

L *is for . . .* LEAVE IT TO COOK: *put it in the oven or on top of the stove and forget about it – until the cooking time is up and it's ready for the table*

Leave it to Cook

BOSTON BAKED BEANS

IMPERIAL/METRIC	AMERICAN
1½ lb. (¾ kilo) dried haricot beans, soaked overnight and drained	*1½ lb. dried navy beans, soaked overnight and drained*
1 lb. (½ kilo) lean belly pork, cut into two pieces	*1 lb. lean bacon, cut into two pieces*
8 oz. (200 grms.) bacon bones	*8 oz. bacon bones*
2 tablespoons molasses	*2 tablespoons molasses*
2 teaspoons dry mustard	*2 teaspoons dry mustard*
2 onions, finely chopped	*2 onions, finely chopped*
salt and pepper	*salt and pepper*

METHOD

Put the beans in a saucepan with fresh water and bring to the boil. Simmer for about 1 hour. Drain, reserving the cooking liquid. Slash the rind of the pieces of belly pork. Place one piece in the bottom of a large casserole and add the beans and bacon bones. Bury the second piece of pork in the beans so that the rind just shows. Stir the molasses, mustard, onions and seasoning into the reserved bean cooking liquid and pour into the casserole. Add more boiling water if necessary to cover the beans. Put the lid on the casserole and bake in a low oven, 300°F, Gas Mark 2, for 6 hours. Add more boiling water from time to time so that the beans are kept covered. For the final hour of cooking, remove the lid and bring the pork to the surface.

Serves 6 to 8.

Boston baked beans

Brigade pudding

BRIGADE PUDDING

IMPERIAL/METRIC	AMERICAN
Pastry	Pastry
8 oz. (200 grms.) self-raising flour	*2 cups self-rising flour*
pinch of salt	*pinch of salt*
4 oz. (100 grms.) shredded suet or butter or margarine	*$\frac{1}{2}$ cup shredded suet or butter or margarine*
water	*water*
Filling	Filling
2 tablespoons golden syrup	*2 tablespoons light corn syrup*
8 oz. (200 grms.) mincemeat	*8 oz. mincemeat*
3 large cooking apples, peeled, cored and grated	*3 large cooking apples, peeled, cored and grated*

METHOD

Sift the flour and salt into a bowl and add the suet or butter or margarine. Rub in well and add enough water to make a soft dough. Roll out the dough thinly and cut into four circles: one the size of the base of a 2 to 3 pint (1 to $1\frac{1}{2}$ litre) or 3 to $3\frac{1}{2}$ pint pudding basin, one a little bigger, another bigger still and finally one almost as large as the rim of the basin. Put the syrup into the greased basin and add the first dough circle. Top with one-third of the mincemeat mixed with one-third of the apple. Continue making layers, ending with the largest dough circle. Cover the basin with greased paper and foil tied on with string. Steam over boiling water for $2\frac{1}{2}$ hours.

Serves 6.

Simple cassoulet

SIMPLE CASSOULET

IMPERIAL/METRIC	AMERICAN
$1\frac{1}{2}$ lb. ($\frac{3}{4}$ kilo) stewing lamb, from the shoulder or blade end, trimmed of excess fat and cut into bite-sized pieces	$1\frac{1}{2}$ lb. stewing lamb, from the shoulder or blade end, trimmed of excess fat and cut into bite-sized pieces
1 onion, sliced	1 onion, sliced
1 oz. (25 grms.) bacon fat	2 tablespoons bacon fat
1 pint ($\frac{1}{2}$ l.) water or stock	$2\frac{1}{2}$ cups water or stock
1 × 5 oz. (125 grms.) can tomato paste	1 × 5 oz. can tomato paste
12 oz. (300 grms.) dried haricot beans, soaked overnight and drained	12 oz. dried navy beans, soaked overnight and drained
2 carrots, sliced	2 carrots, sliced
1 parsnip, sliced	1 parsnip, sliced
2 celery stalks, sliced	2 celery stalks, sliced
parsley sprig	parsley sprig
$\frac{1}{2}$ teaspoon dried thyme	$\frac{1}{2}$ teaspoon dried thyme
1 bay leaf	1 bay leaf
salt and pepper	salt and pepper

METHOD

Brown the lamb and onion in the fat. Stir in a little of the water or stock and the tomato paste. Then add the rest of the water or stock and all the remaining ingredients. Bring gently to the boil, cover and simmer for about 2 hours, or until the meat is tender. Uncover and continue to simmer for a further 30 minutes.
Serves 4.

BEEF GOULASH

IMPERIAL/METRIC	AMERICAN
$1\frac{1}{2}$ lb. ($\frac{3}{4}$ kilo) chuck steak, cut into cubes	$1\frac{1}{2}$ lb. chuck steak, cut into cubes
3 onions, sliced	3 onions, sliced
2 oz. (50 grms.) butter or margarine	$\frac{1}{4}$ cup butter or margarine
$\frac{1}{2}$ pint (250 ml.) stock	$1\frac{1}{4}$ cups stock
1 tablespoon paprika	1 tablespoon paprika
1 lb. ($\frac{1}{2}$ kilo) tomatoes, skinned and chopped	1 lb. tomatoes, skinned and chopped
salt and pepper	salt and pepper
1 lb. ($\frac{1}{2}$ kilo) potatoes, cut into pieces	1 lb. potatoes, cut into pieces
soured cream or plain yogurt	sour cream or plain yogurt
chopped parsley	chopped parsley

METHOD

Brown the meat and onions in the butter or margarine. Mix together the stock and paprika and add to the pan with the tomatoes and seasoning to taste. Simmer gently for $1\frac{3}{4}$ hours, then add the potatoes. Continue cooking for another 45 minutes. Serve topped with soured cream or yogurt and parsley.
Serves 4.

M *is for . . .* MEATLESS MAIN DISHES:
not just for vegetarians, the high price of meat makes these nourishing entrées welcome standbys for every family

Meatless Main Dishes

LENTIL RISSOLES

IMPERIAL/METRIC	AMERICAN
4 oz. (100 grms.) brown or yellow lentils	*4 oz. brown or yellow lentils*
1 large onion, grated	*1 large onion, grated*
2 medium-sized potatoes, cooked and mashed	*2 medium-sized potatoes, cooked and mashed*
3 oz. (75 grms.) fresh breadcrumbs	*1 cup fresh breadcrumbs*
4 oz. (100 grms.) blanched almonds, finely chopped	*$\frac{2}{3}$ cup finely chopped blanched almonds*
1 oz. (25 grms.) sesame seeds	*$\frac{1}{3}$ cup sesame seeds*
salt	*salt*
2 tablespoons chopped parsley	*2 tablespoons chopped parsley*
1 egg, beaten	*1 egg, beaten*

METHOD

Put the lentils in a saucepan and cover with water. Bring to the boil, cover and simmer until tender. Drain and mash the lentils, then mix them with the onion, potatoes, breadcrumbs, nuts, sesame seeds, salt, parsley, beaten egg and enough cold water to bind together. Form the mixture into 12 patties and place them on a greased baking sheet. Bake in a moderate oven, 350°F, Gas Mark 4, for 25 minutes.
Serves 6.

Lentil rissoles

SPANISH RICE

IMPERIAL/METRIC	AMERICAN
1 onion, chopped	*1 onion, chopped*
1 tablespoon oil	*1 tablespoon oil*
$\frac{1}{2}$ oz. (12$\frac{1}{2}$ grms.) butter or margarine	*1 tablespoon butter or margarine*
8 oz. (200 grms.) long-grain rice	*1$\frac{1}{3}$ cups long-grain rice*
1 pint ($\frac{1}{2}$ l.) chicken stock	*2$\frac{1}{2}$ cups chicken stock*
pinch of ground saffron	*pinch of ground saffron*
1 green pepper, pith and seeds removed and chopped	*1 green pepper, pith and seeds removed and chopped*
1 red pepper, pith and seeds removed and chopped	*1 red pepper, pith and seeds removed and chopped*
2 tomatoes, skinned and chopped	*2 tomatoes, skinned and chopped*
salt and pepper	*salt and pepper*
4 oz. (100 grms.) peeled prawns	*4 oz. peeled baby shrimp*

METHOD

Fry the onion in the oil and butter or margarine until soft. Add the rice and cook gently, stirring, for 2 to 3 minutes. Stir in the stock, saffron and green and red peppers. Bring to the boil, cover and cook for about 20 minutes or until all the liquid has been absorbed. Add the tomatoes, seasoning to taste and the prawns (shrimp) and mix well. Cook gently, stirring, for about 5 minutes.
Serves 3 to 4.

PIPERADE

IMPERIAL/METRIC	AMERICAN
2 onions, sliced	*2 onions, sliced*
1 garlic clove, crushed	*1 garlic clove, crushed*
1 green pepper, pith and seeds removed and sliced	*1 green pepper, pith and seeds removed and sliced*
1 red pepper, pith and seeds removed and sliced	*1 red pepper, pith and seeds removed and sliced*
2 oz. (50 grms.) butter or margarine	*¼ cup butter or margarine*
8 oz. (200 grms.) tomatoes, skinned and quartered	*8 oz. tomatoes, skinned and quartered*
6 eggs	*6 eggs*
salt and pepper	*salt and pepper*

METHOD

Fry the onions, garlic and green and red peppers in the butter or margarine until tender. Add the tomatoes and cook for 5 minutes longer, stirring occasionally. Meanwhile, beat the eggs together with seasoning to taste. Pour the eggs into the pan and cook gently until they are slightly scrambled.

Serves 2 to 3.

CAULIFLOWER BASKET

IMPERIAL/METRIC	AMERICAN
1 cauliflower	*1 cauliflower*
1 oz. (25 grms.) butter or margarine	*2 tablespoons butter or margarine*
1 oz. (25 grms.) flour	*¼ cup flour*
½ pint (250 ml.) milk	*1¼ cups milk*
salt and pepper	*salt and pepper*
4 oz. (100 grms.) Cheddar cheese, grated	*1 cup grated Cheddar cheese*
2 hard-boiled eggs, chopped	*2 hard-boiled eggs, chopped*
1 tablespoon chopped gherkins	*1 tablespoon chopped gherkins*
1 teaspoon capers	*1 teaspoon capers*
1 tablespoon chopped parsley	*1 tablespoon chopped parsley*
1 tablespoon chopped chives	*1 tablespoon chopped chives*

METHOD

Cook the cauliflower in boiling salted water until it is tender.

Meanwhile, melt the butter or margarine in a saucepan. Stir in the flour and cook, stirring, for 1 minute. Gradually add the milk, stirring constantly, and bring to the boil. Cook until the sauce thickens. Add seasoning to taste, almost all the cheese, and the remaining ingredients.

Scoop out the centre part of the cauliflower, chop it coarsely and add to the sauce. Place the cauliflower on a hot serving dish and pile the sauce in the centre. Sprinkle with the remaining cheese and brown for 2 to 3 minutes under a hot grill (broiler).

Serves 4.

VEGETABLE CASSEROLE

IMPERIAL/METRIC	AMERICAN
2 large onions, chopped	*2 large onions, chopped*
2 garlic cloves, chopped	*2 garlic cloves, chopped*
vegetable oil for frying	*vegetable oil for frying*
2 green peppers, pith and seeds removed and chopped	*2 green peppers, pith and seeds removed and chopped*
1 lb. (½ kilo) courgettes, sliced	*1 lb. zucchini, sliced*
2 medium-sized aubergines, chopped	*2 medium-sized eggplants, chopped*
8 oz. (200 grms.) mushrooms	*8 oz. mushrooms*
1 lb. (½ kilo) tomatoes, skinned and chopped	*1 lb. tomatoes, skinned and chopped*
1 × 5 oz. (125 grms.) can tomato paste	*1 × 5 oz. can tomato paste*
2 bay leaves	*2 bay leaves*
1 tablespoon chopped parsley	*1 tablespoon chopped parsley*
½ teaspoon dried oregano	*½ teaspoon dried oregano*
½ teaspoon dried thyme	*½ teaspoon dried thyme*
2 large potatoes, thinly sliced	*2 large potatoes, thinly sliced*
1 oz. (25 grms.) butter or margarine	*2 tablespoons butter or margarine*

METHOD

Fry the onions and garlic in oil until soft. Add the green peppers, courgettes (zucchini), aubergines (eggplants) and mushrooms and cook, stirring, for 5 minutes. Transfer the vegetables to a casserole and add the tomatoes, tomato paste and all the herbs. Arrange the potato slices on top in a thick overlapping layer and dot with pieces of butter or margarine. Bake in a moderate oven, 350°F, Gas Mark 4, for about 1 hour or until the potatoes are soft underneath and crisp and brown on top.

Serves 4.

Cauliflower basket

French onion tart

FRENCH ONION TART

IMPERIAL/METRIC	AMERICAN
Pastry	Pastry
8 oz. (200 grms.) wholemeal flour	*2 cups wholemeal flour*
4 oz. (100 grms.) butter or margarine	*½ cup butter or margarine*
water	*water*
Filling	Filling
2 lb. (1 kilo) onions, thinly sliced	*2 lb. onions, thinly sliced*
2 oz. (50 grms.) butter or margarine	*¼ cup butter or margarine*
1 tablespoon oil	*1 tablespoon oil*
salt and pepper	*salt and pepper*
pinch of grated nutmeg	*pinch of grated nutmeg*
2 eggs, beaten	*2 eggs, beaten*
¼ pint (125 ml.) double or soured cream	*⅝ cup heavy or sour cream*

METHOD

To make the pastry, put the flour in a bowl and add the butter or margarine. Rub in until the mixture resembles breadcrumbs. Add enough water to make a soft dough. Chill.

Meanwhile make the filling. Cook the onions gently in the butter or margarine and oil, covered, for about 30 minutes or until they are very soft but not brown.

Roll out the dough, which may be crumbly, and line an 8 inch (20 cm.) flan tin.

Season the onions and add the nutmeg. Allow to cool then stir in the eggs and cream. Pour the onion mixture into the flan case and bake in a fairly hot oven, 375°F, Gas Mark 5, for 35 to 45 minutes or until set. Leave to stand for 5 minutes before serving.

Serves 6.

N *is for . . .* NIGHT BEFORE: *pre-preparation is the answer to effortless meal-planning and entertaining . . .* NUTS FOR NOURISHMENT: *full of protein, nuts can be used in many delicious ways – some of which may surprise you*

Night Before

MUSHROOMS VINAIGRETTE

IMPERIAL/METRIC
6 tablespoons olive oil
2 tablespoons lemon juice
1 garlic clove, crushed
salt and pepper
1 tablespoon finely chopped parsley
8 oz. (200 grms.) mushrooms

AMERICAN
6 tablespoons olive oil
2 tablespoons lemon juice
1 garlic clove, crushed
salt and pepper
1 tablespoon finely chopped parsley
8 oz. mushrooms

METHOD
Mix together the oil, lemon juice, garlic, seasoning and parsley. Pour this dressing over the mushrooms and toss well. Chill.
Serves 4.

Mushrooms vinaigrette

ITALIAN LEMON WATER ICE

IMPERIAL/METRIC
8 oz. (200 grms.) sugar
1 pint (½ l.) water
thinly pared rind of 2 lemons
½ pint (250 ml.) lemon juice
1 egg white (optional)

AMERICAN
1 cup sugar
2½ cups water
thinly pared rind of 2 lemons
1¼ cups lemon juice
1 egg white (optional)

METHOD
Dissolve the sugar in the water, stirring occasionally. Add the lemon rind and boil gently for 10 minutes. Cool. Stir in the lemon juice and strain into an ice cube tray. Place in the freezing compartment of the refrigerator and leave for about 1 hour or until half frozen. Turn the mixture into a bowl and whisk well. If you like, beat the egg white until it is stiff and fold it into the lemon mixture. Return to the ice cube tray and re-freeze. Serve in glasses or in the empty lemon caps.
Serves 6.

Soused fish

SOUSED FISH

IMPERIAL/METRIC	AMERICAN
6 herrings, backbones removed	*6 herrings, backbones removed*
1 onion, sliced	*1 onion, sliced*
vinegar	*vinegar*
water	*water*
4 bay leaves	*4 bay leaves*
2 cloves	*2 cloves*
12 allspice berries	*12 allspice berries*
2 mace blades	*2 mace blades*
1 teaspoon salt	*1 teaspoon salt*

METHOD

Lay the herrings, skin sides down, on a working surface and place sliced onion on the centre of each fish. Roll up the fish from head to tail and secure with wooden toothpicks. Place the fish rolls in an ovenproof dish and add vinegar and water to cover in the proportion of three parts vinegar to one part water. Add the herbs, spices and salt. Cover the dish and cook in a low oven, 300°F, Gas Mark 2, for 3 hours or until the fish is cooked. The liquid must not boil. Transfer the fish to a serving dish and strain the cooking liquid over. Chill – the liquid will set to a jelly. Garnish with black olives and pickled cucumber slices and serve with potato and cucumber salads.

Serves 6.

GAZPACHO

IMPERIAL/METRIC	AMERICAN
2 lb. (1 kilo) tomatoes, skinned	*2 lb. tomatoes, skinned*
½ cucumber, peeled and finely diced	*½ cucumber, peeled and finely diced*
1 green pepper, pith and seeds removed and diced	*1 green pepper, pith and seeds removed and diced*
1 red pepper, pith and seeds removed and diced	*1 red pepper, pith and seeds removed and diced*
6 shallots, thinly sliced	*6 scallions, thinly sliced*
1 tablespoon olive oil	*1 tablespoon olive oil*
1 tablespoon wine vinegar	*1 tablespoon wine vinegar*
8 fl. oz. (200 ml.) chilled water	*1 cup chilled water*
1 garlic clove, crushed	*1 garlic clove, crushed*
salt and pepper	*salt and pepper*
1 hard-boiled egg yolk, sieved	*1 hard-boiled egg yolk, sieved*
ice cubes	*ice cubes*

METHOD

Purée the tomatoes in a liquidizer or push them through a sieve with a wooden spoon. Add all the remaining ingredients, except the egg yolk and ice cubes, and stir well. Chill. Just before serving, garnish with the egg yolk and add ice cubes.

Serves 6.

SPINACH PANCAKES WITH TOMATO SAUCE

IMPERIAL/METRIC	AMERICAN
Batter	Batter
6 oz. (150 grms.) flour	*$1\frac{1}{2}$ cups flour*
$\frac{1}{4}$ teaspoon salt	*$\frac{1}{4}$ teaspoon salt*
1 egg	*1 egg*
$\frac{3}{4}$ pint (375 ml.) milk	*2 cups milk*
fat for frying	*fat for frying*
Filling	Filling
1 lb. ($\frac{1}{2}$ kilo) fresh spinach	*1 lb. fresh spinach*
8 oz. (200 grms.) cottage cheese	*8 oz. cottage cheese*
3 eggs, lightly beaten	*3 eggs, lightly beaten*
2 oz. (50 grms.) grated Parmesan cheese	*$\frac{1}{3}$ cup grated Parmesan cheese*
grated nutmeg	*grated nutmeg*
Tomato sauce	Tomato sauce
2 large onions, finely chopped	*2 large onions, finely chopped*
2 garlic cloves, crushed	*2 garlic cloves, crushed*
4 tablespoons olive oil	*4 tablespoons olive oil*
1 × 5 oz. (125 grms.) can tomato paste	*1 × 5 oz. can tomato paste*
1 × 15 oz. (375 grms.) can tomatoes	*1 × 15 oz. can tomatoes*
2 bay leaves	*2 bay leaves*
4 tablespoons chopped parsley	*4 tablespoons chopped parsley*
$\frac{1}{4}$ teaspoon dried oregano	*$\frac{1}{4}$ teaspoon dried oregano*
small piece lemon rind	*small piece lemon rind*
salt	*salt*
4 tablespoons water	*4 tablespoons water*

METHOD

To make the batter, sift the flour and salt into a bowl. Add the egg and half the milk and whisk to a smooth paste. Gradually beat in the remaining milk. Heat fat in a frying-pan or crêpe pan. When it is hot pour off any excess. Drop 2 to 3 tablespoons of the batter into the centre of the pan and quickly tilt the pan so that the bottom is completely covered with the batter. Cook for 1 minute, then turn the pancake over and cook for another minute. Turn the pancake out of the pan on to a plate. Cook more pancakes in the same way, stacking them with a piece of greaseproof (waxed) paper between them.

To make the filling, wash the spinach thoroughly and put it in a saucepan. There should be enough water left on the leaves so that you need not add any more. Cook the spinach for 7 to 10 minutes or until it is just tender. Drain, pressing out all the excess water, and chop the spinach. Mix in the cottage cheese, eggs, cheese and a pinch of nutmeg. Spread each pancake with a little of the spinach mixture and roll them up. Arrange the rolled pancakes in a greased ovenproof dish and chill.

Spinach pancakes with tomato sauce

For the sauce, fry the onions and garlic in the oil until soft. Stir in the tomato paste, tomatoes, bay leaves, parsley, oregano, lemon rind, salt and water. Simmer gently for 1 to $1\frac{1}{2}$ hours, stirring occasionally. Chill.

To serve, brush the top layer of rolled pancakes with a little melted butter or margarine and sprinkle with a little Parmesan cheese. Bake in a moderate oven, 350°F, Gas Mark 4, for 20 minutes or until heated through. Reheat the tomato sauce and pour over the rolled and stuffed pancakes.

Serves 4 to 6.

ARGENTINE BEEF STEW

IMPERIAL/METRIC
- 2 onions, chopped
- 1 large red pepper, pith and seeds removed and diced
- $1\frac{1}{2}$ lb. ($\frac{3}{4}$ kilo) chuck steak, cut into $\frac{1}{2}$ inch ($1\frac{1}{4}$ cm.) cubes
- 2 tablespoons olive oil
- 2 pints (1 l.) beef stock
- 2 teaspoons paprika
- 4 bacon rashers, diced
- 8 oz. (200 grms.) red or garlic sausage, sliced
- 4 oz. (100 grms.) dried butter beans, soaked overnight and drained
- salt and pepper
- 1 × $7\frac{1}{2}$ oz. (200 grms.) can sweetcorn, drained

AMERICAN
- 2 onions, chopped
- 1 large red pepper, pith and seeds removed and diced
- $1\frac{1}{2}$ lb. chuck steak, cut into $\frac{1}{2}$ inch cubes
- 2 tablespoons olive oil
- 5 cups beef stock
- 2 teaspoons paprika
- 4 bacon slices, diced
- 8 oz. red or garlic sausage, sliced
- $\frac{3}{4}$ cup dried lima beans, soaked overnight and drained
- salt and pepper
- 1 × $7\frac{1}{2}$ oz. can corn, drained

METHOD

Fry the onions, red pepper and meat in the oil until the meat cubes are browned. Stir in the stock, paprika, bacon, sausage, beans and seasoning to taste. Bring to the boil, cover tightly and simmer gently for about 2 hours. Allow to cool and chill. To serve, add the sweetcorn, bring to the boil and simmer for 30 minutes.
Serves 6.

VEAL WITH TUNA SAUCE

IMPERIAL/METRIC
- $1\frac{1}{2}$ lb. ($\frac{3}{4}$ kilo) cold roast veal, preferably boneless
- $\frac{1}{2}$ pint (250 ml.) thick mayonnaise
- 1 × 7 oz. (175 grms.) can tuna, finely mashed with its oil
- juice of $\frac{1}{2}$ lemon
- 8 anchovy fillets, finely chopped
- 1 tablespoon finely chopped capers (optional)
- pepper
- veal or chicken stock
- lemon wedges, anchovy fillets and capers to garnish

AMERICAN
- $1\frac{1}{2}$ lb. cold roast veal, preferably boneless
- $1\frac{1}{4}$ cups thick mayonnaise
- 1 × 7 oz. can tuna, finely mashed with its oil
- juice of $\frac{1}{2}$ lemon
- 8 anchovy fillets, finely chopped
- 1 tablespoon finely chopped capers (optional)
- pepper
- veal or chicken stock
- lemon wedges, anchovy fillets and capers to garnish

Argentine beef stew

METHOD

Slice the veal fairly thinly and arrange the slices on a large serving dish. Mix together the mayonnaise, tuna, lemon juice, chopped anchovy fillets, capers and pepper to taste. Thin down the sauce to the consistency of cream with veal or chicken stock. Pour the sauce over the veal and chill. Garnish just before serving.
Serves 6 to 8.

Veal with tuna sauce

Biscotten torte

BISCOTTEN TORTE

IMPERIAL/METRIC	AMERICAN
4 oz. (100 grms.) butter or margarine	*½ cup butter or margarine*
4 oz. (100 grms.) castor sugar	*½ cup superfine sugar*
2 eggs	*2 eggs*
4 oz. (100 grms.) ground almonds	*⅔ cup ground almonds*
few drops almond essence	*few drops almond extract*
½ pint (250 ml.) milk	*1¼ cups milk*
1½ tablespoons rum	*1½ tablespoons rum*
12 oz. (300 grms.) plain sweet oblong biscuits	*12 oz. plain sweet oblong cookies*
½ pint (250 ml.) whipping cream, whipped	*1¼ cups whipping cream, whipped*
toasted, slivered almonds	*toasted, slivered almonds*

METHOD

Cream the butter or margarine and sugar together until light and fluffy. Separate the eggs and beat the yolks into the creamed mixture. Add the ground almonds, almond essence and half the milk. Beat the egg whites until they are stiff, then fold them into the almond mixture. Mix the rum and remaining milk together.

Arrange six biscuits (cookies) lengthways in two rows – three biscuits (cookies) to a row – beside each other on a sheet of greaseproof (waxed) paper. Brush them generously with the milk and rum mixture. Spread with one-third of the almond filling. Continue with brushed biscuits (cookies) and filling, ending with a row of biscuits (cookies). Wrap securely in aluminium foil and refrigerate for several hours, preferably overnight. Just before serving, cover the torte with whipped cream and decorate with almonds.

Serves 6.

Nuts for Nourishment

STUFFED PEACHES

IMPERIAL/METRIC	AMERICAN
6 oz. (150 grms.) cream cheese	*6 oz. cream cheese*
2 tablespoons sultanas, soaked in boiling water for 5 minutes and drained	*2 tablespoons golden raisins, soaked in boiling water for 5 minutes and drained*
2 tablespoons chopped walnuts	*2 tablespoons chopped walnuts*
2 ripe peaches or 4 canned peach halves	*2 ripe peaches or 4 canned peach halves*
lettuce leaves	*lettuce leaves*

METHOD

Mix the cheese, sultanas (raisins) and nuts together and make into 12 small balls. Arrange the peach halves on lettuce leaves in four individual bowls or glasses and place three cheese balls on each. Chill.

Serves 4.

PEANUT SAUCE FOR VEGETABLES

IMPERIAL/METRIC	AMERICAN
8 oz. (200 grms.) crunchy peanut butter	*8 oz. crunchy peanut butter*
3 tablespoons soya sauce	*3 tablespoons soy sauce*
juice of ½ lemon	*juice of ½ lemon*
1 teaspoon honey	*1 teaspoon honey*
2 garlic cloves, crushed	*2 garlic cloves, crushed*

METHOD

Mix all the ingredients together in a saucepan with enough water to make a thick pouring sauce. Heat the sauce but do not boil.

POTATO ALMOND BALLS

IMPERIAL/METRIC	AMERICAN
8 oz. (200 grms.) potatoes, cooked and mashed	*8 oz. potatoes, cooked and mashed*
3 oz. (75 grms.) blanched almonds, finely chopped	*½ cup finely chopped blanched almonds*
1 egg, beaten	*1 egg, beaten*
oil or fat for frying	*oil or fat for frying*

METHOD

Mix the potatoes with about one-third of the nuts. Form into small balls. Coat with the beaten egg and the rest of the nuts. Fry in hot oil or fat until crisp and golden brown.

Serves 2 to 3.

Stuffed peaches

Syrian fruit salad

SYRIAN FRUIT SALAD

IMPERIAL/METRIC	AMERICAN
4 oz. (100 grms.) prunes	*$\frac{2}{3}$ cup prunes*
4 oz. (100 grms.) dried apricots	*$\frac{2}{3}$ cup dried apricots*
4 oz. (100 grms.) dried figs	*$\frac{2}{3}$ cup dried figs*
2 oz. (50 grms.) raisins	*$\frac{1}{3}$ cup raisins*
2 oz. (50 grms.) blanched almonds	*$\frac{1}{3}$ cup blanched almonds*
2 oz. (50 grms.) walnuts	*$\frac{1}{3}$ cup walnuts*
2 oz. (50 grms.) pine nuts	*$\frac{1}{3}$ cup pine nuts*
2 tablespoons rosewater	*2 tablespoons rosewater*
2 tablespoons sugar dissolved in 1 tablespoon water	*2 tablespoons sugar dissolved in 1 tablespoon water*

METHOD

Soak the dried fruit in water to cover for 48 hours. Add all the remaining ingredients and stir gently. Chill.
Serves 6 to 8.

Sauteed crab with almonds

SAUTEED CRAB WITH ALMONDS

IMPERIAL/METRIC	AMERICAN
3 oz. (75 grms.) butter or margarine	*$\frac{3}{8}$ cup butter or margarine*
1 lb. ($\frac{1}{2}$ kilo) fresh crabmeat	*1 lb. fresh crabmeat*
4 oz. (100 grms.) blanched almonds, split in half	*4 oz. blanched almonds, split in half*
salt and pepper	*salt and pepper*
$\frac{1}{4}$ pint (125 ml.) plain yogurt or soured cream	*$\frac{5}{8}$ cup plain yogurt or sour cream*
2 tablespoons chopped parsley	*2 tablespoons chopped parsley*

METHOD

Melt half the butter or margarine in a frying-pan. Add the crabmeat and toss lightly until delicately browned. In another frying-pan, brown the almonds in the remaining butter or margarine. Add the seasoning and crabmeat to the almonds. Stir in the yogurt or sour cream and parsley and simmer for 2 minutes.
Serves 4.

O is for . . . OLD FAVOURITES: *just like Mother used to make, and popular today, too* . . . ON YOUR OWN: *if you live alone, you may not often take the trouble to cook for yourself, but these dishes will surely tempt you*

Old Favourites

STEAK AND KIDNEY PIES

IMPERIAL/METRIC	AMERICAN
12 oz. (300 grms.) stewing steak, cut in ½ inch (1¼ cm.) cubes	*12 oz. stewing steak, cut in ½ inch cubes*
4 oz. (100 grms.) ox kidney, cut in ½ inch (1¼ cm.) cubes	*4 oz. ox kidney, cut in ½ inch cubes*
2 tablespoons flour	*2 tablespoons flour*
salt and pepper	*salt and pepper*
1 large onion, finely chopped	*1 large onion, finely chopped*
1 oz. (25 grms.) lard	*2 tablespoons cooking fat*
½ pint (250 ml.) beef stock	*1¼ cups beef stock*
Pastry	Pastry
12 oz. (300 grms.) flour	*3 cups flour*
¼ teaspoon salt	*¼ teaspoon salt*
4 oz. (100 grms.) butter or margarine	*½ cup butter or margarine*
3 oz. (75 grms.) lard	*⅜ cup shortening*
water	*water*
beaten egg or milk	*beaten egg or milk*

METHOD

Toss the steak and kidney cubes in the seasoned flour. Fry the onion in the lard (cooking fat) until just tender. Add the steak and kidney cubes and brown well. Stir in the stock and seasoning to taste and bring to the boil. Cover and simmer for about 2 hours or until the meat is tender. Cool.

To make the pastry, sift the flour and salt into a bowl. Add the butter or margarine and lard (shortening) and rub in until the mixture resembles breadcrumbs. Add enough water to make a firm dough. Roll out two-thirds of the dough and cut out six 5½ inch (14 cm.) circles. Line six 4 inch (10 cm.) diameter patty tins with the dough circles. Roll out the remaining dough and cut out six 4 inch (10 cm.) circles for lids. Divide the steak and kidney mixture between the six tins. Cover with the dough lids and pinch the edges together to seal. Use any dough trimmings to decorate the tops of the pies. Glaze with beaten egg or milk. Bake in a fairly hot oven, 400°F, Gas Mark 6, for 25 to 30 minutes or until the pastry is cooked and golden brown.

Serves 6.

Steak and kidney pies

KILLARNEY HOT POT

IMPERIAL/METRIC	AMERICAN
8 oz. (200 grms.) belly of pork or fairly fat ham, cut into pieces	*8 oz. belly of pork or fairly fat ham, cut into pieces*
1 lb. ($\frac{1}{2}$ kilo) lean brisket or chuck steak, cut into pieces	*1 lb. lean brisket or chuck steak, cut into pieces*
salt and pepper	*salt and pepper*
2 teaspoons chopped fresh rosemary or $\frac{1}{4}$ teaspoon dried rosemary	*2 teaspoons chopped fresh rosemary or $\frac{1}{4}$ teaspoon dried rosemary*
$1\frac{1}{2}$ lb. ($\frac{3}{4}$ kilo) potatoes, thinly sliced	*$1\frac{1}{2}$ lb. potatoes, thinly sliced*
1 lb. ($\frac{1}{2}$ kilo) onions, thinly sliced	*1 lb. onions, thinly sliced*
3 large carrots, sliced	*3 large carrots, sliced*
8 oz. (200 grms.) tomatoes, skinned and sliced	*8 oz. tomatoes, skinned and sliced*
$\frac{1}{4}$ pint (125 ml.) brown ale	*$\frac{5}{8}$ cup brown ale*
1 oz. (25 grms.) butter or margarine	*2 tablespoons butter or margarine*

METHOD

Mix together the meat, seasoning and rosemary. Arrange about one-third of the potato slices in the bottom of a casserole. Add half the onions, carrots and tomatoes, half the meat and then another layer of potatoes. Season each layer of vegetables. Add the remainder of the meat and vegetables and pour in the brown ale. Arrange the remaining potato slices on top in a neat overlapping design. Dot the top with small pieces of butter or margarine. Cook in a warm oven, 325°F, Gas Mark 3, for about 2 hours or until the meat is tender. Put the lid on the casserole after the first 15 minutes (this allows the butter or margarine to melt first and thus prevents the lid from sticking), but remove it again for the last 20 minutes to allow the potatoes to brown and crisp.

Serves 4 to 5.

CHICKEN PIE

IMPERIAL/METRIC	AMERICAN
Pastry	Pastry
8 oz. (200 grms.) flour	*2 cups flour*
pinch of salt	*pinch of salt*
6 oz. (150 grms.) butter or margarine	*$\frac{3}{4}$ cup butter or margarine*
water	*water*
beaten egg	*beaten egg*
Filling	Filling
1 × 3 lb. ($1\frac{1}{2}$ kilos) chicken	*1 × 3 lb. chicken*
1 onion, chopped	*1 onion, chopped*
1 bouquet garni	*1 bouquet garni*
8 oz. (200 grms.) mushrooms	*8 oz. mushrooms*
2 oz. (50 grms.) butter or margarine	*$\frac{1}{4}$ cup butter or margarine*
1 oz. (25 grms.) flour	*$\frac{1}{4}$ cup flour*
1 tablespoon chopped parsley	*1 tablespoon chopped parsley*
salt and pepper	*salt and pepper*
4 tablespoons double cream	*4 tablespoons heavy cream*
2 tablespoons white wine (optional)	*2 tablespoons white wine (optional)*

METHOD

To make the pastry, sift the flour and salt into a bowl. Add the butter or margarine and cut it into small pieces. Add enough water to make a soft dough. Roll out the dough to an oblong on a lightly floured board. Fold the dough in three like an envelope and turn it so that the open end is facing you. Roll out again, fold and turn. Repeat the rolling, folding and turning once more. Chill.

Put the chicken, onion and bouquet garni into a large saucepan. Add enough water to cover and bring to the boil. Cover with a tight-fitting lid and simmer for about 1 hour or until the chicken is tender. Remove the chicken from the stock and allow to cool. Strain the stock and reserve about $\frac{1}{2}$ pint (250 ml.) or $1\frac{1}{4}$ cups.

Fry the mushrooms in the butter or margarine until just tender. Stir in the flour and cook, stirring, for 1 minute. Gradually add the reserved chicken stock, stirring constantly. Bring to the boil and simmer for 2 to 3 minutes, stirring, or until the mixture thickens. Stir in the parsley, seasoning, cream and wine, if used. Remove from the heat and set aside.

Take the chicken meat off the carcass, remove the skin and cut the meat into bite-sized pieces. Put the chicken meat, in alternating layers with the mushroom mixture, in a 2 pint (1 litre) or 5 cup pie dish. Leave until completely cold.

Roll out the dough to about $\frac{1}{4}$ inch ($\frac{3}{4}$ cm.) thickness and large enough to cover the pie dish with a $\frac{1}{2}$ inch ($1\frac{1}{4}$ cm.) border. Cut $\frac{1}{2}$ inch ($1\frac{1}{4}$ cm.) border from the dough, dampen the rim of the pie dish and press the border strip on to it. Place a pie funnel in the centre of the pie dish and lay the dough over the top, pressing firmly on to the border strip to seal. Crimp the edge and use the dough trimming to decorate the top. Brush with beaten egg. Bake in a hot oven, 425°F, Gas Mark 7, for 25 to 35 minutes or until the pastry is risen and golden brown.

Serves 6.

MAIDS OF HONOUR

IMPERIAL/METRIC	AMERICAN
Pastry	Pastry
6 oz. (150 grms.) flour	*1½ cups flour*
pinch of salt	*pinch of salt*
4 oz. (100 grms.) butter or margarine	*½ cup butter or margarine*
water	*water*
Filling	Filling
jam	*jam*
6 oz. (150 grms.) cottage cheese, sieved	*6 oz. cottage cheese, sieved*
2 oz. (50 grms.) sultanas	*⅓ cup golden raisins*
½ teaspoon almond essence	*½ teaspoon almond extract*
2 tablespoons ground or finely chopped almonds	*2 tablespoons ground or finely chopped almonds*
2 eggs	*2 eggs*
Topping	Topping
4 oz. (100 grms.) icing sugar, sifted	*⅔ cup confectioners' sugar, sifted*
water	*water*
few drops almond essence	*few drops almond extract*

METHOD

To make the pastry, sift the flour and salt into a bowl. Add one-third of the butter or margarine and rub in until the mixture resembles breadcrumbs. Add enough water to make an elastic dough. Roll out to an oblong on a lightly floured board. Cut the remaining fat into small pieces. Dot two-thirds of the dough with half the fat pieces. Bring up the uncovered dough third and fold in three like an envelope. Turn the pastry so that the open end faces you and roll out again into an oblong. Repeat with the remaining fat, fold and turn. Roll out, fold and chill.

Roll out the dough until it is wafer-thin. Cut out 12 to 15 circles to line fairly deep 3 inch (7½ cm.) diameter patty tins. Put a teaspoon of jam into each tin. Mix together all the remaining filling ingredients, beating well. Spoon into the pastry cases over the jam. Bake in a hot to very hot oven, 450 to 475°F, Gas Mark 7 to 8, for 10 minutes. Reduce the oven temperature to moderate, 350°F, Gas Mark 4, and bake for a further 15 minutes. Allow to cool.

For the topping, blend the icing (confectioners') sugar with enough water to make a flowing consistency. Mix in the almond essence (extract). Spoon a little on to each little cake and leave to set.

Makes 12 to 15.

APPLE PAN DOWDY

IMPERIAL/METRIC	AMERICAN
3 large cooking apples	*3 large cooking apples*
2 tablespoons brown sugar	*2 tablespoons brown sugar*
2 tablespoons golden syrup	*2 tablespoons light corn syrup*
grated nutmeg	*grated nutmeg*
ground cinnamon	*ground cinnamon*
Batter	Batter
4 oz. (100 grms.) self-raising flour	*1 cup self-rising flour*
pinch of salt	*pinch of salt*
2 oz. (50 grms.) sugar	*¼ cup sugar*
1 egg	*1 egg*
4 tablespoons milk	*4 tablespoons milk*
2 oz. (50 grms.) butter or margarine, melted	*¼ cup butter or margarine, melted*

METHOD

Peel and slice the apples into a greased 1½ pint (1 litre) or 2 pint pie dish. Sprinkle with the brown sugar, syrup, nutmeg and cinnamon. Cover the dish with aluminium foil and bake in a moderate oven, 350°F, Gas Mark 4, for 15 to 20 minutes or until the apples are nearly soft.

Meanwhile, to make the batter sift the flour and salt into a bowl. Add all the remaining ingredients and mix well to make a thick batter. Remove the foil from the apples and spoon the batter over them. Sprinkle lightly with sugar and bake for a further 30 to 35 minutes. Turn the pudding upside-down on to a warm serving dish.

Serves 4.

Apple pan dowdy

On Your Own

BARBECUED BEEF SATE

IMPERIAL/METRIC	AMERICAN
6 to 8 oz. (150 to 200 grms.) rump steak	*6 to 8 oz. rump steak*
1 tablespoon soya sauce	*1 tablespoon soy sauce*
1 teaspoon honey	*1 teaspoon honey*
½ garlic clove, crushed	*½ garlic clove, crushed*
¼ teaspoon ground coriander	*¼ teaspoon ground coriander*
¼ teaspoon caraway seeds	*¼ teaspoon caraway seeds*
pinch of chilli powder	*pinch of chilli powder*
1 tablespoon vegetable oil	*1 tablespoon vegetable oil*

METHOD

Cut the steak into 1 inch (2½ cm.) cubes and place them in a bowl. Mix the remaining ingredients together and pour over the meat. Marinate for 1 hour, stirring occasionally. Thread the meat on to two skewers. Grill (broil) or barbecue over hot coals on a small barbecue (hibachi) for 10 minutes, turning occasionally. Baste with the marinade during cooking.

FRIED LIVER WITH ORANGE

IMPERIAL/METRIC	AMERICAN
1 tablespoon flour	*1 tablespoon flour*
salt and pepper	*salt and pepper*
grated rind of ½ small orange	*grated rind of ½ small orange*
4 oz. (100 grms.) lamb's liver, sliced	*4 oz. lamb's liver, sliced*
1 oz. (25 grms.) butter or margarine	*2 tablespoons butter or margarine*
juice of ½ small orange	*juice of ½ small orange*

METHOD

Mix together the flour, seasoning and orange rind. Coat the liver slices with this mixture. Melt the butter or margarine in a frying-pan and fry the liver for about 5 minutes, turning once. Be careful not to overcook the liver. Pour over the orange juice and mix well with the pan juices. Simmer for 1 to 2 minutes longer.

MACKEREL SALAD

IMPERIAL/METRIC	AMERICAN
few lettuce leaves	*few lettuce leaves*
1 × 4½ oz. (112½ grms.) can mackerel fillets	*1 × 4½ oz. can mackerel fillets*
3 tablespoons mayonnaise	*3 tablespoons mayonnaise*
1½ teaspoons horseradish sauce	*1½ teaspoons horseradish sauce*
few capers	*few capers*
2 gherkins, chopped	*2 gherkins, chopped*
2 tomatoes, quartered	*2 tomatoes, quartered*
paprika	*paprika*

Barbecued beef sate

METHOD

Arrange the lettuce leaves on a plate. Drain the mackerel fillets and place them on the lettuce. Mix together the mayonnaise, horseradish sauce, capers and gherkins and spoon over the mackerel fillets. Put the tomato quarters around the edge, and sprinkle with paprika.

RUMANIAN HERB OMELET

IMPERIAL/METRIC

3 eggs
salt and pepper
4 tablespoons yogurt or soured cream
2 tablespoons flour, sifted
1 tablespoon finely chopped fresh sorrel, tarragon, parsley or chives
$\frac{1}{2}$ oz. ($12\frac{1}{2}$ grms.) butter or margarine

AMERICAN

3 eggs
salt and pepper
4 tablespoons yogurt or sour cream
2 tablespoons flour, sifted
1 tablespoon finely chopped fresh sorrel, tarragon, parsley or chives
1 tablespoon butter or margarine

METHOD

Beat the eggs lightly with a fork and season to taste. Whisk in the yogurt or sour cream, flour and herbs. Melt the butter or margarine in a heavy-based frying-pan or omelet pan and pour in the egg mixture. Cook over low heat, moving the omelet around to prevent it burning. When golden brown underneath, turn it over and cook the other side. Slide the omelet on to a warm plate and top with a nut of butter or margarine.

Rumanian herb omelet

FRIED BANANA WITH RUM

IMPERIAL/METRIC

1 large banana
$\frac{1}{2}$ oz. ($12\frac{1}{2}$ grms.) butter
squeeze of lemon juice
1 tablespoon rum
sugar

AMERICAN

1 large banana
1 tablespoon butter
squeeze of lemon juice
1 tablespoon rum
sugar

METHOD

Peel the banana and cut it in half lengthways. Cook gently in the butter for about 2 minutes, turning once. Add the lemon juice and rum (first warmed in a ladle and then flamed). Sprinkle with sugar.

P is for . . . PICNICS AND BARBECUES: *somehow food tastes better and appetites increase in the open air . . .* PRESERVES AND PICKLES: *make your own to treat your family and friends – and use the produce from your own garden*

Picnics and Barbecues

BAKED HAM

IMPERIAL/METRIC	AMERICAN
½ leg of ham weighing approx. 5 lb. (2½ kilos)	*½ leg of ham weighing approx. 5 lb.*
dry mustard	*dry mustard*
cloves	*cloves*
8 fl. oz. (200 ml.) cider	*1 cup cider*
4 tablespoons brown sugar	*4 tablespoons brown sugar*
pineapple rings	*pineapple rings*
maraschino cherries	*maraschino cherries*

METHOD

Remove the skin from the ham and rub it with dry mustard. Stud the fat side with cloves. Place the ham on a rack in a roasting tin and bake in a hot oven, 425°F, Gas Mark 7, for 20 minutes. Reduce the oven temperature to moderate, 350°F, Gas Mark 4, and pour the cider over the ham. Bake for a further 1 hour 20 minutes, basting occasionally. Sprinkle half the brown sugar over the ham and bake for a further 30 minutes without basting. During the last 15 minutes, place the pineapple rings around the ham and sprinkle with the remaining brown sugar. Place the ham on a carving board and garnish with the glazed pineapple rings and maraschino cherries. Allow to cool and refrigerate.

Serves 10 to 12.

Baked ham

STUFFED PICNIC LOAF

IMPERIAL/METRIC	AMERICAN
4 tomatoes, skinned and chopped	*4 tomatoes, skinned and chopped*
4 shallots or spring onions, chopped	*4 shallots or scallions, chopped*
1 green pepper, pith and seeds removed and chopped	*1 green pepper, pith and seeds removed and chopped*
12 black olives, stoned and chopped	*12 black olives, stoned and chopped*
1 tablespoon capers	*1 tablespoon capers*
2 dill pickled cucumbers, chopped	*2 dill pickled cucumbers, chopped*
1 large French loaf	*1 large French loaf*
olive oil	*olive oil*
½ teaspoon dried basil	*½ teaspoon dried basil*
salt	*salt*
freshly ground black pepper	*freshly ground black pepper*

METHOD

Combine the tomatoes, shallots or spring onions (scallions), green pepper, olives, capers and pickled cucumbers. Cut the French loaf in half lengthways and scoop out all the bread. Mix the crumbled bread with the tomato mixture, a little olive oil, basil, salt and pepper. Fill the two empty bread crust shells with the mixture, press together, wrap the loaf securely in aluminium foil and chill. This is best if made the day before.

Serves 4.

MEAT LOAF

IMPERIAL/METRIC	AMERICAN
½ oz. (12½ grms.) butter or margarine	*1 tablespoon butter or margarine*
2 oz. (50 grms.) dry breadcrumbs	*1 cup dry breadcrumbs*
2 lb. (1 kilo) lean minced beef, or mixed beef and pork or beef sausage meat	*2 lb. lean ground beef or mixed beef and pork or beef sausage meat*
1 onion, finely chopped	*1 onion, finely chopped*
salt and pepper	*salt and pepper*
½ stock cube dissolved in 1 tablespoon boiling water	*½ stock cube, dissolved in 1 tablespoon boiling water*
dash of garlic salt	*dash of garlic salt*
¼ teaspoon mixed dried herbs	*¼ teaspoon mixed dried herbs*
2 tablespoons tomato purée	*2 tablespoons tomato purée*
1 egg	*1 egg*

METHOD

Grease a 2-pound (1 kilo) loaf tin with the butter or margarine and coat it with some of the breadcrumbs. Mix the remaining ingredients together thoroughly, using your hands. Pack the mixture into the loaf tin and bake in a fairly hot oven, 375°F, Gas Mark 5, for 1¼ hours. Cool and refrigerate.
Serves 6 to 8.

BARBECUED SAUSAGE

IMPERIAL/METRIC	AMERICAN
2 lb. (1 kilo) pork sausages, pricked	*2 lb. pork sausages, pricked*
4 celery stalks, chopped	*4 celery stalks, chopped*
2 onions, chopped	*2 onions, chopped*
butter or margarine	*butter or margarine*
4 tablespoons vinegar	*4 tablespoons vinegar*
½ pint (250 ml.) tomato sauce	*1 ¼ cups tomato sauce*
4 tablespoons water	*4 tablespoons water*
1 tablespoon brown sugar	*1 tablespoon brown sugar*
1 tablespoon prepared mustard	*1 tablespoon prepared mustard*
1 teaspoon Worcestershire sauce	*1 teaspoon Worcestershire sauce*

METHOD

Cook the sausages on the barbecue or grill (broil) them until they are cooked. Meanwhile, fry the celery and onions in butter or margarine until tender. Add all the remaining ingredients and mix well. Bring to the boil and add the cooked sausages. Simmer for 15 minutes.
Serves 4 to 6.

BARBECUED CHICKEN DRUMSTICKS

IMPERIAL/METRIC	AMERICAN
2 tablespoons oil or melted butter or margarine	*2 tablespoons oil or melted butter or margarine*
1 teaspoon prepared mustard	*1 teaspoon prepared mustard*
few drops Worcestershire sauce	*few drops Worcestershire sauce*
6 chicken drumsticks	*6 chicken drumsticks*

METHOD

Mix together the oil or melted butter or margarine, mustard and Worcestershire sauce. Brush the drumsticks with this mixture and cook them over the barbecue, with sausages, tomatoes, and jacket potatoes.
Serves 4 to 6.

Honey cheesecake

HONEY CHEESECAKE

IMPERIAL/METRIC	AMERICAN
8 oz. (200 grms.) wheatmeal biscuits	*8 oz. graham crackers*
2 oz. (50 grms.) butter or margarine, melted	*¼ cup butter or margarine, melted*
12 oz. (300 grms.) cottage cheese	*12 oz. cottage cheese*
4 oz. (100 grms.) honey	*½ cup honey*
2 teaspoons sugar	*2 teaspoons sugar*
pinch of salt	*pinch of salt*
2 eggs	*2 eggs*
ground cinnamon	*ground cinnamon*

METHOD

Crush the biscuits (crackers) between two sheets of greaseproof (waxed) paper. Put into a bowl and mix in the melted butter or margarine. Line the base and sides of an 8-inch (20-cm.) cake tin with the crumb mixture. Allow to set for 1 hour in a cool place.

Beat together the cottage cheese, honey, sugar, salt and eggs until the mixture is smooth. Put into the crumb shell, sprinkle liberally with cinnamon and bake in a low oven, 300°F, Gas Mark 2, for 45 minutes. Cool.
Serves 6 to 8.

Barbecued chicken drumstic

Preserves and Pickles

PEAR AND GINGER PRESERVE

IMPERIAL/METRIC	AMERICAN
4 lb. (2 kilos) pears (about 12 pears)	*4 lb. pears (about 12 pears)*
1 tablespoon lemon juice	*1 tablespoon lemon juice*
6 cloves	*6 cloves*
$2\frac{1}{4}$ lb. (1 kilo 50 grms.) sugar	*$4\frac{1}{2}$ cups sugar*
$1\frac{1}{4}$ pints (625 ml.) water	*3 cups water*
4 oz. (100 grms.) preserved ginger, in syrup	*4 oz. preserved ginger, in syrup*
rind of 1 orange, cut into matchstick-thin strips	*rind of 1 orange, cut into matchstick-thin strips*

METHOD

Peel, core and slice the pears into a dish. Add the lemon juice and cloves and let stand for about 30 minutes.

Meanwhile, put the sugar and water in a preserving pan. Bring to the boil, stirring until the sugar dissolves, then boil for 8 minutes. Add the pears to the syrup and simmer gently until the pears are tender and the syrup quite thick.

Chop the ginger into small pieces and add with the orange rind to the pears. Stir well and bring to the boil again. Pour the hot preserve into hot clean jars and cover immediately with a well-fitting waxed paper disc and then with a cellophane, parchment or thin polythene cover, fastened with string or rubber bands.

Makes about 7 pounds ($3\frac{1}{4}$ kilograms).

MIXED VEGETABLE PICKLE

IMPERIAL/METRIC	AMERICAN
1 cauliflower, broken into flowerets	*1 cauliflower, broken into flowerets*
1 cucumber, peeled and cut into $\frac{1}{2}$ inch ($1\frac{1}{4}$ cm.) dice	*1 cucumber, peeled and cut into $\frac{1}{2}$ inch dice*
1 lb. ($\frac{1}{2}$ kilo) French beans, cut into 1 inch ($2\frac{1}{2}$ cm.) lengths	*1 lb. green beans, cut into 1 inch lengths*
8 oz. (200 grms.) small pickling onions	*8 oz. baby onions*
salt	*salt*
Spiced Vinegar	Spiced Vinegar
2 pints (1 l.) malt vinegar malt vinegar	*5 cups malt vinegar*
cinnamon stick	*cinnamon stick*
12 cloves	*12 cloves*
4 mace blades	*4 mace blades*
15 allspice berries	*15 allspice berries*
8 peppercorns	*8 peppercorns*

METHOD

Put the cauliflower flowerets, cucumber dice, bean pieces and onions in layers in a bowl, sprinkling each layer with salt. Cover with a clean towel and leave for 48 hours.

To make the vinegar, put the malt vinegar and spices in a heatproof bowl over a saucepan of cold water. Cover the bowl with a plate. Bring the water to the boil, then remove the pan from the heat and allow the spices to steep in the warm vinegar for about 2 hours. Strain.

Drain the vegetables, rinse off excess salt and pack loosely in clean jars, arranging the different vegetables attractively. Fill the jars with the spiced vinegar and seal with vinegar-proof covers.

TOMATO RELISH

IMPERIAL/METRIC	AMERICAN
3 lb. ($1\frac{1}{2}$ kilos) ripe tomatoes, skinned and roughly chopped	*3 lb. ripe tomatoes, skinned and roughly chopped*
1 large onion, finely chopped	*1 large onion, finely chopped*
3 celery stalks, finely chopped	*3 celery stalks, finely chopped*
salt	*salt*
2 teaspoons curry powder	*2 teaspoons curry powder*
1 tablespoon flour	*1 tablespoon flour*
$\frac{1}{2}$ teaspoon dry mustard	*$\frac{1}{2}$ teaspoon dry mustard*
1 pint ($\frac{1}{2}$ l.) white malt vinegar	*$2\frac{1}{2}$ cups white malt vinegar*
12 oz. (300 grms.) sugar	*$1\frac{1}{2}$ cups sugar*

METHOD

Put the tomatoes, onion and celery in a bowl and sprinkle them with salt. Cover with a clean towel and leave for 24 hours.

Mix the curry powder, flour and mustard together. Add enough of the vinegar to make a paste. Drain the vegetables, rinse off the excess salt and put them in an enamel or stainless steel pan. Heat gently until simmering then cook for 5 minutes. Dissolve the sugar in the remaining vinegar and add to the pan. Simmer for 30 minutes. Stir in the flour paste and cook for a further 2 to 3 minutes, stirring constantly. Pour into hot clean jars and cover with vinegar-proof covers.

Makes about 4 pounds (2 kilograms).

Pear and ginger preserve

Chocolate fondue

Q *is for . . .* QUICK DESSERTS: *when you have only a few minutes to whip up something sweet, these desserts will fit the bill*

Quick Desserts

CHOCOLATE FONDUE

IMPERIAL/METRIC	AMERICAN
8 oz. (200 grms.) dark sweet chocolate	*8 oz. (8 squares) dark sweet chocolate*
6 tablespoons double cream	*6 tablespoons heavy cream*
2 tablespoons rum or brandy	*2 tablespoons rum or brandy*
3 oz. (75 grms.) chopped blanched almonds	*½ cup chopped blanched almonds*
fresh or canned fruit, sponge or lady fingers, cubes of sponge cake, marshmallows, etc. for dipping	*fresh or canned fruit, sponge or lady fingers, cubes of sponge cake, marshmallows, etc. for dipping*

METHOD

Break the chocolate into small pieces and put into a saucepan with the cream. Stir over gentle heat until the chocolate melts. Blend in the rum or brandy and nuts. Pour the chocolate mixture into a shallow earthenware fondue pot and place it over the spirit flame. Serve with the fruit and cake for dipping.

Serves 3 to 4.

STRAWBERRY WHIP

IMPERIAL/METRIC	AMERICAN
1½ pints (¾ l.) milk	*3¾ cups milk*
1 lb. (½ kilo) strawberries	*1 lb. strawberries*
4 generous tablespoons vanilla ice cream	*4 generous tablespoons vanilla ice cream*
2 oz. (50 grms.) sugar	*¼ cup sugar*
1 teaspoon vanilla essence or 1 tablespoon brandy	*1 teaspoon vanilla extract or 1 tablespoon brandy*
ice cubes	*ice cubes*
¼ pint (125 ml.) whipping cream, whipped	*⅝ cup whipping cream, whipped*
strawberries to garnish	*strawberries to garnish*

METHOD

Blend the milk, strawberries, ice cream, sugar and vanilla or brandy together in a liquidiser. Pour on to ice cubes in four tall glasses. Top with whipped cream and whole strawberries. To make without a liquidiser, purée the strawberries by pushing them through a fine sieve or strainer, then beat all the ingredients together with a whisk or egg beater.

Serves 4.

Strawberry whip

SYLLABUB

IMPERIAL/METRIC	AMERICAN
$\frac{1}{2}$ pint (250 ml.) double cream	*$1\frac{1}{4}$ cups heavy cream*
1 to 2 oz. (25 to 50 grms.) icing sugar, sifted	*$\frac{1}{6}$ to $\frac{1}{3}$ cup confectioners' sugar, sifted*
juice of 1 lemon	*juice of 1 lemon*
up to $\frac{1}{4}$ pint (125 ml.) white wine	*up to $\frac{5}{8}$ cup white wine*

METHOD

Beat the cream until it begins to stand in peaks. Do not overbeat until it is stiff. Beat in the sugar to taste, the lemon juice and as much of the wine as you like. The mixture will be very soft. Spoon it into glasses or small dishes and chill. Serve with fingers of sponge cake or sweet biscuits (cookies).

Serves 4.

FRESH FRUIT SALAD

IMPERIAL/METRIC	AMERICAN
$\frac{1}{2}$ pint (250 ml.) water	*$1\frac{1}{4}$ cups water*
2 oranges	*2 oranges*
1 lemon	*1 lemon*
3 to 4 oz. (75 to 100 grms.) sugar	*$\frac{3}{8}$ to $\frac{1}{2}$ cup sugar*
2 lb. (1 kilo) mixed prepared fresh fruit	*2 lb. mixed prepared fresh fruit*

METHOD

Put the water with thin strips of the orange and lemon rind into a saucepan. Simmer for 5 minutes. Add the sugar, stir until dissolved, then add the orange and lemon juice. Strain over the fruit and allow to become cold.

Serves 4 to 6.

Fresh fruit salad

R *is for* . . . REHEATABLE: *some dishes improve if made the day before and reheated – the flavours are more concentrated and rich* . . . REFRESHING SALADS: *in warm weather nothing is more appetising than a crisp or creamy salad*

Reheatable

Ratatouille

RATATOUILLE

IMPERIAL/METRIC

1 large aubergine
1 lb. ($\frac{1}{2}$ kilo) courgettes, sliced
salt and pepper
4 medium-sized onions, sliced
1 to 2 garlic cloves, finely chopped
4 tablespoons olive oil
1 green pepper, pith and seeds removed and sliced
1 red pepper, pith and seeds removed and sliced
1 lb. ($\frac{1}{2}$ kilo) ripe tomatoes skinned and chopped
parsley to garnish

AMERICAN

1 large eggplant
1 lb. zucchini, sliced
salt and pepper
4 medium-sized onions, sliced
1 to 2 garlic cloves, finely chopped
4 tablespoons olive oil
1 green pepper, pith and seeds removed and sliced
1 red pepper, pith and seeds removed and sliced
1 lb. ripe tomatoes, skinned and chopped
parsley to garnish

METHOD

Roughly chop or slice the aubergine (eggplant) into a bowl and add the courgettes (zucchini). Sprinkle with salt and pepper and leave for 30 minutes. This removes the bitter taste and draws out excess water from the vegetables. Fry the onions and garlic in the oil until soft and translucent. Add all the remaining vegetables and stir well. Simmer gently, covered, for about 25 to 30 minutes or until the vegetables are just tender. Serve immediately or reheat as follows: cool and store, covered, in the refrigerator. Cook in a moderate oven, 350°F, Gas Mark 4, in a covered casserole for 30 minutes and garnish with parsley. Ratatouille may also be served cold.

Serves 4 to 6.

BLACKBERRY AND APPLE PIE

IMPERIAL/METRIC	AMERICAN
Pastry	Pastry
8 oz. (200 grms.) flour	*2 cups flour*
4 oz. (100 grms.) butter or margarine	*½ cup butter or margarine*
1 tablespoon castor sugar	*1 tablespoon superfine sugar*
1 egg yolk	*1 egg yolk*
water	*water*
Filling	Filling
1 lb. (½ kilo) cooking apples	*1 lb. cooking apples*
1 box blackberries	*1 box blackberries*
¼ teaspoon ground cinnamon	*¼ teaspoon ground cinnamon*
sugar	*sugar*

METHOD

Sift the flour into a bowl. Add the butter or margarine and rub in until the mixture resembles fine breadcrumbs. Add the sugar and egg yolk and enough water to make a firm dough. Roll out half the dough into a circle and line an 8 to 9 inch (20 to 22½ cm.) pie dish.

Peel, core and slice the apples. Mix them with the blackberries, adding the cinnamon and sugar to taste. Spoon the fruit mixture into the pie dish. Brush the edge of the dough with cold water. Roll out the remaining dough to a circle and place it on top of the pie dish. Seal the edges, trim neatly and decorate the edge. Make a hole in the centre with a skewer to allow the steam to escape. Sprinkle with a little sugar and bake towards the top of a hot oven, 425°F, Gas Mark 7, for 30 to 40 minutes, or until the pastry is golden brown. Serve immediately with cream, or reheat as follows: cool and store, covered, in a cool place. Reheat in a moderate oven, 350°F, Gas Mark 4, for 20 to 30 minutes. For variation, use 1½ lb. (600 grms.) apples, gooseberries, raspberries, cherries or apricots in the pie.

Serves 6 to 8.

Blackberry and apple pie

CHICKEN WITH APRICOTS

IMPERIAL/METRIC	AMERICAN
3 to 3½ lb. (1½ kilos) chicken	*3 to 3½ lb. chicken*
3 tablespoons oil	*3 tablespoons oil*
1 tablespoon flour	*1 tablespoon flour*
1 pint (½ l.) apricot juice (from soaked fruit)	*2½ cups apricot juice (from soaked fruit)*
1 onion, finely chopped	*1 onion, finely chopped*
2 teaspoons sugar	*2 teaspoons sugar*
salt and pepper	*salt and pepper*
1 lb. (½ kilo) dried apricots, soaked overnight	*1 lb. dried apricots, soaked overnight*

METHOD

Cut the chicken meat off the carcass in bite-sized pieces. Fry the pieces in the oil until they are golden. Remove them from the pan and keep warm. Pour off all but 1 tablespoon oil from the pan. Stir in the flour and gradually add ½ pint (1¼ cups) of the apricot juice, stirring constantly. Stir in the onion and simmer for 5 minutes.

Return the chicken pieces to the pan with the sugar, seasoning to taste, the apricots and the remaining apricot juice. The chicken should be covered with liquid, so if necessary add more apricot juice or water. Bring to the boil and simmer, covered, for about 20 minutes or until the chicken pieces are tender. Serve immediately or reheat as follows: cool and store, covered, in the refrigerator. Bring to the boil and simmer, covered, for about 20 minutes or until the chicken pieces are heated through.

Serves 4.

Chicken with apricots

CAULIFLOWER PANCAKE GATEAU

IMPERIAL/METRIC

Batter
4 oz. (100 grms.) flour
pinch of salt
1 egg
½ pint (250 ml.) mixed milk and water
oil for frying

Filling
1 cauliflower
salt
2 oz. (50 grms.) butter or margarine, melted
2 tablespoons double cream
2 tablespoons chopped chives

AMERICAN

Batter
1 cup flour
pinch of salt
1 egg
1¼ cups mixed milk and water
oil for frying

Filling
1 cauliflower
salt
¼ cup butter or margarine, melted
2 tablespoons heavy cream
2 tablespoons chopped chives

METHOD

Sift the flour and salt into a large bowl. Add the egg and half the milk and water mixture and mix to a smooth paste. Gradually beat in the remaining liquid. Heat a little oil in a frying-pan or crêpe pan. When it is hot, pour off any surplus. Drop 2 to 3 tablespoons of the batter into the centre of the pan and quickly tilt the pan in all directions so that the batter covers the entire bottom. Cook for about 1 minute, then turn the pancake over with a fish slice or palette knife. Cook for about another minute. Turn the pancake out of the pan on to a warm plate. Continue making pancakes in the same way. Keep them hot.

Meanwhile, break the cauliflower into flowerets and cook in boiling salted water for 10 to 15 minutes, or until tender. Drain the flowerets and mash them roughly with a fork. Blend in half the melted butter or margarine and the cream. Spread each pancake with the cauliflower filling and pile them on top of each other. Pour the remaining melted butter or margarine over the top and sprinkle with the chives. Serve immediately, or reheat as follows: cool the pancake gâteau and store, covered, in the refrigerator. Reheat in a fairly hot oven, 375°F, Gas Mark 5, for 40 minutes and then pour over the remaining melted butter and chives.

Serves 4 to 6.

ROULADEN

IMPERIAL/METRIC

3 lb. (1 ½ kilos) silverside of beef, thinly sliced
2 to 4 oz. (50 to 100 grms.) speck (fat ham)
German mustard
1 dill pickled cucumber, cut lengthways into eight segments
2 onions, finely chopped
salt and pepper
1 carrot, sliced
2 oz. (50 grms.) dripping
2 oz. (50 grms.) flour
1 pint (½ l.) water

AMERICAN

3 lb. beef rump roast, thinly sliced
2 to 4 oz. speck (fat ham)
German mustard
1 dill pickled cucumber, cut lengthways into eight segments
2 onions, finely chopped
salt and pepper
1 carrot, sliced
¼ cup dripping
½ cup flour
2½ cups water

METHOD

Beat the meat slices with a cleaver, meat mallet or rolling pin to make them very thin. Cut out eight 4 × 8 inch (10 × 20 cm.) rectangles. Use the remaining meat in a stew or casserole or soup. Cut the speck into eight long strips. Spread each rectangle of meat with mustard, place a strip of speck and a cucumber segment across the centre, sprinkle with half the chopped onion, salt and pepper and roll up tightly. Secure the rolls with cotton thread or wooden toothpicks. Fry the remaining onion and the carrot in the dripping in a shallow heavy-based pan until golden. Coat the meat rolls with the flour and fry with the vegetables until evenly browned. Add the water and bring to the boil, stirring occasionally.

Transfer to a casserole and cook in a moderate oven, 350°F, Gas Mark 4, for 1 hour or until the meat is tender. Serve immediately or reheat as follows: cool and store, covered, in the refrigerator. Bring to the boil on top of the stove then reheat in a moderate oven, 350°F, Gas Mark 4, for 30 minutes. Place the rouladen on a bed of hot mashed potatoes. Strain the gravy, pour a little over the rolls and serve the rest in a sauceboat.

Serves 6 to 8.

Refreshing Salads

GREEK SALATA

IMPERIAL/METRIC	AMERICAN
½ small red cabbage, shredded	*½ small red cabbage, shredded*
4 oz. (100 grms.) cooked beetroot, cut in julienne strips	*⅔ cup cooked beet, cut in julienne strips*
4 oz. (100 grms.) cooked green beans	*⅔ cup cooked green beans*
1 tablespoon capers	*1 tablespoon capers*
1 tablespoon chopped olives	*1 tablespoon chopped olives*
Dressing	Dressing
3 tablespoons olive oil	*3 tablespoons olive oil*
1 tablespoon wine vinegar	*1 tablespoon wine vinegar*
1 teaspoon sugar	*1 teaspoon sugar*
½ teaspoon dry mustard	*½ teaspoon dry mustard*
½ teaspoon salt	*½ teaspoon salt*
freshly ground black pepper	*freshly ground black pepper*
1 garlic clove, crushed	*1 garlic clove, crushed*

METHOD

Place the cabbage, beetroot (beets) and beans in a salad bowl. Sprinkle over the capers and olives. Put all the dressing ingredients in a screw-top jar and shake well. Pour the dressing over the salad and toss. Chill for at least 30 minutes before serving.

Serves 6 to 8.

Greek salata

Blue cheese and pear salad

BLUE CHEESE AND PEAR SALAD

IMPERIAL/METRIC	AMERICAN
8 oz. (200 grms.) blue cheese, crumbled	*8 oz. blue cheese, crumbled*
mayonnaise	*mayonnaise*
8 canned or fresh pear halves	*8 canned or fresh pear halves*
lettuce	*lettuce*
grapes	*grapes*
chopped nuts	*chopped nuts*

METHOD

Blend the crumbled cheese with enough mayonnaise to make a creamy consistency. Arrange the pear halves on a bed of lettuce. Top with the cheese mixture, garnish with grapes and sprinkle with nuts.

Serves 4.

HERRING SALAD

IMPERIAL/METRIC	AMERICAN
4 medium-sized herrings, filleted	*4 medium-sized herrings, filleted*
salt and pepper	*salt and pepper*
oil	*oil*
1 small onion, finely chopped	*1 small onion, finely chopped*
1 sweet apple, cored and finely chopped	*1 sweet apple, cored and finely chopped*
2 teaspoons sherry	*2 teaspoons sherry*
3 tablespoons mayonnaise	*3 tablespoons mayonnaise*
$\frac{1}{4}$ teaspoon curry powder	*$\frac{1}{4}$ teaspoon curry powder*
1 tablespoon tomato purée	*1 tablespoon tomato purée*
3 tablespoons plain yogurt	*3 tablespoons plain yogurt*
1 carrot, grated	*1 carrot, grated*
1 hard-boiled egg, chopped	*1 hard-boiled egg, chopped*
lettuce	*lettuce*
watercress	*watercress*
lemon slices	*lemon slices*

METHOD

Season the herrings and brush them with a little oil. Grill (broil) carefully so the flesh does not break. Be sure not to overcook them. Cool, then chop the herrings into neat pieces. Blend one herring with the onion (reserving about 1 teaspoon), apple and sherry. Blend a second herring with the mayonnaise and curry powder. Blend the third herring with the tomato purée and yogurt. And blend the fourth herring with the carrot, egg and reserved onion. Arrange the four mixtures on a bed of lettuce and watercress. Garnish with lemon slices.

Serves 4 to 6.

Herring salad

WALNUT AND AVOCADO SALAD

IMPERIAL/METRIC	AMERICAN
2 ripe avocado pears	*2 ripe avocados*
lemon juice	*lemon juice*
2 crisp sweet apples, peeled, cored and chopped	*2 crisp sweet apples, peeled, cored and chopped*
2 oz. (50 grms.) walnuts, chopped	*$\frac{1}{3}$ cup chopped walnuts*
lettuce leaves	*lettuce leaves*
cucumber slices	*cucumber slices*
Dressing	Dressing
3 tablespoons olive oil	*3 tablespoons olive oil*
1 tablespoon wine vinegar	*1 tablespoon wine vinegar*
1 teaspoon sugar	*1 teaspoon sugar*
$\frac{1}{2}$ teaspoon dry mustard	*$\frac{1}{2}$ teaspoon dry mustard*
$\frac{1}{2}$ teaspoon salt	*$\frac{1}{2}$ teaspoon salt*
freshly ground black pepper	*freshly ground black pepper*
1 garlic clove, crushed	*1 garlic clove, crushed*

METHOD

Cut the avocados carefully in half and remove the stone. Scrape the flesh gently into a bowl without damaging the skins. Mash the flesh and sprinkle it with lemon juice to prevent it turning brown. Stir in the apples and walnuts. Put all the dressing ingredients in a screw-top jar and shake well. Blend the dressing into the avocado mixture, and spoon it back into the avocado skins. Arrange the filled avocado halves on lettuce leaves and garnish with cucumber slices. Serve immediately.
Serves 4.

SWEET AND SOUR CHICKEN SALAD

IMPERIAL/METRIC	AMERICAN
1 small cooked chicken	*1 small cooked chicken*
2 tablespoons blanched flaked almonds	*2 tablespoons blanched flaked almonds*
endive or lettuce	*curly endive or lettuce*
sliced cooked beetroot	*sliced cooked beets*
sliced cooked potatoes	*sliced cooked potatoes*
Marinade	Marinade
2 teaspoons French mustard	*2 teaspoons French mustard*
4 tablespoons white wine vinegar	*4 tablespoons white wine vinegar*
6 tablespoons salad oil	*6 tablespoons salad oil*
2 garlic cloves, crushed	*2 garlic cloves, crushed*
1 teaspoon soya sauce	*1 teaspoon soy sauce*
1 tablespoon honey	*1 tablespoon honey*
salt and pepper	*salt and pepper*
8 small pickled gherkins or 2 pickled cucumbers, sliced	*8 small pickled gherkins or 2 pickled cucumbers, sliced*
4 canned pineapple rings, chopped	*4 canned pineapple rings, chopped*
1 tablespoon seedless raisins	*1 tablespoon seedless raisins*

Sweet and sour chicken salad

METHOD

Cut the chicken meat off the carcass in small neat pieces. To make the marinade, blend the mustard with the vinegar, then add the oil, garlic, soya sauce, honey and seasoning. Stir in the gherkins or cucumbers, pineapple, raisins and the pieces of chicken. Allow to marinate for 15 minutes, then stir in the nuts.

Arrange the endive or lettuce on a serving plate. Pile the chicken mixture in the centre and garnish with the beetroot (beet) and potato slices.
Serves 6.

S *is for . . .* SPICING IT UP: *ring the changes and add an aromatic spice or two to sweet or savoury dishes . . .* SOUPS TO MAKE A MEAL: *a hearty soup with bread and cheese will satisfy a hungry family for lunch or supper*

Spicing it Up

WALNUT SPICE SANDWICH CAKE

IMPERIAL/METRIC	AMERICAN
3 oz. (75 grms.) flour	*¾ cup flour*
pinch of salt	*pinch of salt*
1 teaspoon mixed spice	*1 teaspoon mixed spice*
3 eggs	*3 eggs*
3 oz. (75 grms.) castor sugar	*⅜ cup superfine sugar*
1 oz. (25 grms.) finely chopped walnuts	*3 tablespoons finely chopped walnuts*
½ pint (250 ml.) double cream, whipped	*1¼ cups heavy cream, whipped*
walnut halves	*walnut halves*

METHOD

Sift the flour, salt and spice two or three times on to a plate or piece of greaseproof (waxed) paper. Put the eggs into a double boiler or a bowl placed over a pan of hot water and beat with a balloon whisk or electric beater until pale yellow and thick. Add the sugar and continue beating until the mixture trebles in volume and becomes the consistency of softly whipped cream. This will take about 10 minutes with a whisk and 5 minutes with an electric beater. Sprinkle the walnuts and flour mixture over the top and gently and lightly cut and fold them into the egg mixture using a metal spoon. When evenly combined, carefully spoon the batter into two 7 inch (17½ cm.) sandwich tins (layer cake pans) which have been lined with greaseproof (waxed) paper and greased. Bake in the centre of a moderate oven, 350°F, Gas Mark 4, for 15 to 20 minutes or until the cakes are well risen and golden. Turn out on to a towel-covered wire rack and peel away the paper. When completely cold, sandwich together with the whipped cream and decorate the top with walnut halves.

Serves 8.

BEEF CURRY

IMPERIAL/METRIC	AMERICAN
1 tablespoon ground coriander	*1 tablespoon ground coriander*
1 teaspoon ground turmeric	*1 teaspoon ground turmeric*
½ teaspoon cumin	*½ teaspoon cumin*
¼ teaspoon chilli powder	*¼ teaspoon chilli powder*
pinch of ground cinnamon	*pinch of ground cinnamon*
2 cloves	*2 cloves*
1 bay leaf	*1 bay leaf*
3 tablespoons vinegar	*3 tablespoons vinegar*
1 onion, chopped	*1 onion, chopped*
1 garlic clove, crushed	*1 garlic clove, crushed*
2 tablespoons vegetable oil	*2 tablespoons vegetable oil*
1 lb. (½ kilo) beef topside, cut into 1 inch (2½ cm.) cubes	*1 lb. beef chuck steak, cut into 1 inch (2½ cm.) cubes*
1 teaspoon salt	*1 teaspoon salt*
¼ pint (125 ml.) water	*⅝ cup water*
1 beef stock cube, crumbled	*1 beef stock cube, crumbled*

METHOD

Mix and pound the spices with the vinegar to form a paste. Fry the onion and garlic in the oil for 5 minutes. Add the spice paste and fry, stirring, for 2 minutes. Add the beef cubes and cook, stirring occasionally, until the beef is evenly browned. Stir in the remaining ingredients and simmer, covered, for 1 hour.

Serves 4.

Walnut spice sandwich cake

Rice casserole

RICE CASSEROLE

IMPERIAL/METRIC	AMERICAN
1¼ lb. (600 grms.) rice	*3⅓ cups rice*
1 onion, chopped	*1 onion, chopped*
2 garlic cloves, crushed	*2 garlic cloves, crushed*
1 green pepper, pith and seeds removed and chopped	*1 green pepper, pith and seeds removed and chopped*
3 tablespoons olive oil	*3 tablespoons olive oil*
3 carrots, diced	*3 carrots, diced*
8 oz. (200 grms.) young green beans, chopped	*8 oz. young green beans, chopped*
8 oz. (200 grms.) cooked or canned kidney beans	*8 oz. cooked or canned kidney beans*
1 tablespoon chopped parsley	*1 tablespoon chopped parsley*
¼ teaspoon ground saffron	*¼ teaspoon ground saffron*
¼ teaspoon ground turmeric	*¼ teaspoon ground turmeric*
¼ teaspoon crushed coriander	*¼ teaspoon crushed coriander*
1½ pints (¾ l.) vegetable stock	*2 pints vegetable stock*

METHOD

Half cook the rice. Fry the onion, garlic and green pepper in the oil until soft. Stir in the carrots, green and kidney beans, parsley and the half-cooked rice. Mix the saffron, turmeric and coriander into the stock and add slowly to the rice mixture, stirring. Bring to the boil and cook gently, covered, for about 20 minutes or until all the liquid has been absorbed.
Serves 6.

Soups to make a Meal

LENTIL SOUP

IMPERIAL/METRIC	AMERICAN
8 oz. (200 grms.) brown lentils	*8 oz. brown lentils*
2 pints (1 l.) cold water	*$2\frac{1}{2}$ pints cold water*
6 oz. (150 grms.) leek, chopped	*6 oz. leek, chopped*
1 onion, chopped	*1 onion, chopped*
1 carrot, chopped	*1 carrot, chopped*
1 green pepper, pith and seeds removed and chopped	*1 green pepper, pith and seeds removed and chopped*
3 tablespoons oil	*3 tablespoons oil*
1 large tomato, skinned and chopped	*1 large tomato, skinned and chopped*
$1\frac{1}{2}$ oz. (38 grms.) butter or margarine	*3 tablespoons butter or margarine*
3 tablespoons flour	*3 tablespoons flour*
$\frac{1}{2}$ pint (250 ml.) stock	*$1\frac{1}{4}$ cups stock*
2 tablespoons vinegar	*2 tablespoons vinegar*
salt and pepper	*salt and pepper*

METHOD

Put the lentils and water in a large saucepan and bring to the boil. Simmer, covered, for 1 hour. Fry the leek, onion, carrot and green pepper in the oil for 5 minutes. Add to the cooked lentils with the tomato. Melt the butter or margarine in the pan in which the vegetables were fried and stir in the flour. Cook, stirring for 1 minute. Gradually stir in the stock and vinegar and bring to the boil. Simmer, stirring, until the mixture has thickened. Stir the stock mixture into the lentil mixture and season well. Cook gently, stirring occasionally, for a further 30 minutes.

Serves 6.

Lentil soup

MINESTRONE

IMPERIAL/METRIC	AMERICAN
1 large onion, finely chopped	*1 large onion, finely chopped*
2 tablespoons olive oil	*2 tablespoons olive oil*
4 lean bacon rashers, chopped	*4 lean bacon slices, chopped*
1 small white cabbage, shredded	*1 small white cabbage, shredded*
4 celery stalks, chopped	*4 celery stalks, chopped*
3 pints ($1\frac{1}{2}$ l.) beef stock	*$7\frac{1}{2}$ cups beef stock*
2 oz. (50 grms.) dried haricot beans, soaked overnight and drained	*$\frac{1}{4}$ cup dried navy beans, soaked overnight and drained*
salt and pepper	*salt and pepper*
4 large tomatoes, skinned and chopped	*4 large tomatoes, skinned and chopped*
2 tablespoons tomato purée	*2 tablespoons tomato purée*
1 garlic clove, finely chopped	*1 garlic clove, finely chopped*
6 oz. (150 grms.) any other vegetables in season, such as diced marrow, diced aubergine, cauliflower flowerets, diced turnips, diced parsnip, diced swedes, shelled peas or sliced green beans	*1 cup any other vegetables in season, such as diced squash, diced eggplant, cauliflower flowerets, diced turnips, diced parsnip, diced rutabage, shelled peas or sliced green beans*
2 oz. (50 grms.) broken macaroni	*$\frac{1}{2}$ cup broken macaroni*
1 teaspoon dried basil or thyme	*1 teaspoon dried basil or thyme*
grated Parmesan cheese	*grated Parmesan cheese*

METHOD

Fry the onion in the oil in a large saucepan until soft and translucent. Add the bacon and fry for a further 3 minutes. Stir in the cabbage, celery, beef stock and beans and bring to the boil. Season well and simmer, covered, for $2\frac{3}{4}$ hours or until the beans are tender. Add all the remaining ingredients except the cheese and continue to simmer for a further 15 to 20 minutes or until the macaroni is just tender. Serve accompanied with the cheese.

Serves 6.

CHICKEN CHOWDER

IMPERIAL/METRIC	AMERICAN
3 bacon rashers, chopped	*3 bacon slices, chopped*
1 onion, chopped	*1 onion, chopped*
butter or margarine for frying	*butter or margarine for frying*
$\frac{3}{4}$ pint (375 ml.) chicken stock	*2 cups chicken stock*
about 12 oz. (300 grms.) diced root vegetables	*about 2 cups diced root vegetables*
$\frac{1}{2}$ pint (250 ml.) milk	*$1\frac{1}{4}$ cups milk*
about 6 oz. (150 grms.) cooked chicken, diced	*about 1 cup diced cooked chicken*
4 tablespoons sweetcorn	*4 tablespoons corn*
salt and pepper	*salt and pepper*
chopped parsley	*chopped parsley*
paprika	*paprika*

METHOD

Fry the bacon and onion in butter or margarine until the bacon is crisp and the onion soft and translucent. Stir in the stock and bring to the boil. Add the vegetables and cook for about 10 minutes or until they are tender. Stir in the milk, chicken, sweetcorn and seasoning to taste. Simmer for 5 minutes, then serve garnished with parsley and paprika.

Serves 4 to 6.

Minestrone

T is for . . . TIME SAVING: *make-ahead pancakes, crumb crusts for pies, biscuits (cookies) in a creamy dessert, and other quick dishes – tips to save you time*

Time-Saving Tips

Savoury stuffed pancakes

SPEEDY SPICED PATE

IMPERIAL/METRIC	AMERICAN
8 oz. (200 grms.) liverwurst	*8 oz. liverwurst*
4 oz. (100 grms.) cream cheese	*4 oz. cream cheese*
2 tablespoons mayonnaise	*2 tablespoons mayonnaise*
3 tablespoons single cream	*3 tablespoons light cream*
1 teaspoon Worcestershire sauce	*1 teaspoon Worcestershire sauce*
½ teaspoon curry powder	*½ teaspoon curry powder*
1 teaspoon brandy or dry vermouth	*1 teaspoon brandy or dry vermouth*
salt and pepper	*salt and pepper*

METHOD

Mix all the ingredients together thoroughly with seasoning to taste. Chill and serve with hot toast.

Serves 6 to 8.

SAVOURY STUFFED PANCAKES

IMPERIAL/METRIC	AMERICAN
Batter	Batter
4 oz. (100 grms.) flour	*1 cup flour*
salt	*salt*
1 egg	*1 egg*
½ pint (250 ml.) milk	*1¼ cups milk*
fat for frying	*fat for frying*
Filling	Filling
2 oz. (50 grms.) butter or margarine	*¼ cup butter or margarine*
2 oz. (50 grms.) flour	*½ cup flour*
1 pint (½ l.) milk	*2½ cups milk*
salt and pepper	*salt and pepper*
1 × 7½ oz. (178 grms.) can salmon	*1 × 7½ oz. can salmon*
4 spring onions, chopped	*4 scallions, chopped*
2-inch piece cucumber, chopped	*2-inch piece cucumber, chopped*
4 oz. (100 grms.) Cheddar cheese, grated	*1 cup grated Cheddar cheese*

METHOD

Sift the flour and salt into a large bowl. Add the egg and half the milk and mix to a smooth paste. Gradually beat in the remaining milk. Heat a little fat in a frying-pan or crêpe pan. When it is hot, pour off any surplus. Drop 2 to 3 tablespoons of the batter into the centre of the pan and quickly tilt the pan in all directions so that the batter covers the entire bottom. Cook for about 1 minute, then turn the pancake over with a fish slice or palette knife. Cook for about another minute. Turn the pancake out of the pan. Continue making pancakes in the same way, stacking them with a piece of greaseproof (waxed) paper between each.

To make the filling, melt the butter or margarine in a saucepan and stir in the flour. Cook, stirring, for 1 minute. Gradually stir in the milk and cook, stirring, until the sauce comes to the boil and thickens. Season to taste. Add the salmon, together with any juice from the can, the spring onions (scallions) and cucumber to half the sauce. Divide this filling between the pancakes and roll them up. Place the stuffed pancakes in an ovenproof dish. Add the cheese to the remaining sauce and pour it over the pancakes. Bake in a moderately hot oven, 400°F, Gas Mark 6, for 30 minutes.

Serves 4.

Speedy spiced pate

Bangers bolognese

BANGERS BOLOGNESE

IMPERIAL/METRIC	AMERICAN
1 lb. ($\frac{1}{2}$ kilo) pork sausages	*1 lb. pork sausages*
1 large onion, finely chopped	*1 large onion, finely chopped*
1 garlic clove, crushed	*1 garlic clove, crushed*
1 tablespoon oil	*1 tablespoon oil*
1 oz. (25 grms.) butter or margarine	*2 tablespoons butter or margarine*
1 × 6 oz. (150 grms.) can condensed tomato soup	*1 × 6 oz. can condensed tomato soup*
1 × 15 oz. (375 grms.) can tomatoes	*1 × 15 oz. can tomatoes*
1 tablespoon chopped parsley	*1 tablespoon chopped parsley*
salt and pepper	*salt and pepper*
8 oz. (200 grms.) spaghetti	*8 oz. spaghetti*
grated Parmesan cheese	*grated Parmesan cheese*

METHOD

Fry or grill (broil) the sausages until they are cooked. When they are cool enough to handle, cut each diagonally into four. Fry the onion and garlic in the oil and half the butter or margarine until lightly browned. Stir in the tomato soup, tomatoes, parsley and seasoning. Bring to the boil and simmer, uncovered, for 10 minutes. Add the sausages and cook for a further 5 minutes.

Meanwhile, cook the spaghetti in plenty of boiling salted water for about 12 minutes or until it is tender but still firm. Drain well and toss with the remaining butter or margarine. Turn the spaghetti on to a hot serving dish and spoon over the sauce. Sprinkle with the cheese.

Serves 4.

HERB "PATE"

IMPERIAL/METRIC	AMERICAN
6 oz. (150 grms.) cream cheese	*6 oz. cream cheese*
$\frac{1}{4}$ pint (125 ml.) double cream, lightly whipped	*$\frac{5}{8}$ cup heavy cream, lightly whipped*
$\frac{1}{2}$ teaspoon chopped fresh thyme	*$\frac{1}{2}$ teaspoon chopped fresh thyme*
$\frac{1}{2}$ teaspoon chopped fresh dill	*$\frac{1}{2}$ teaspoon chopped fresh dill*
1 teaspoon chopped fresh chives	*1 teaspoon chopped fresh chives*
salt and pepper	*salt and pepper*

METHOD

Blend together the cheese and cream. Stir in the herbs and seasoning. Chill. Serve with crisp biscuits (crackers).

Serves 4.

RICH CHEESECAKE

IMPERIAL/METRIC	AMERICAN
8 oz. (200 grms.) semi-sweet biscuits	*8 oz. graham crackers*
4 oz. (100 grms.) butter or margarine, melted	*$\frac{1}{2}$ cup butter or margarine, melted*
$1\frac{1}{2}$ lb. ($\frac{3}{4}$ kilo) cream or cottage cheese	*$1\frac{1}{2}$ lb. cream or cottage cheese*
6 oz. (150 grms.) castor sugar	*$\frac{3}{4}$ cup superfine sugar*
2 eggs	*2 eggs*
grated rind of 1 lemon	*grated rind of 1 lemon*
1 tablespoon lemon juice	*1 tablespoon lemon juice*
strawberries	*strawberries*

METHOD

Crush the biscuits (crackers) between two sheets of greaseproof (waxed) paper. Put into a bowl and mix in the melted butter or margarine. Line the base and sides of an 8 inch (20 cm.) ovenproof serving dish, or cake tin with a removeable base, with the crumb mixture. Allow to set for 1 hour in a cool place.

Cream the cheese with the sugar and eggs. If using cottage cheese this may be sieved first. Beat in the lemon rind and juice. Arrange halved strawberries on the bottom of the crumb case and spoon over the cheese mixture. Smooth the top. Bake in the centre of a cool oven, 300°F, Gas Mark 2, for 30 to 40 minutes or until the filling is set. Turn off the oven, but leave the cheesecake inside until it is cold (this prevents it wrinkling). Chill and decorate with more halved strawberries.

Serves 6 to 8.

GINGER CREAM ROLL

IMPERIAL/METRIC	AMERICAN
$\frac{1}{4}$ pint (125 ml.) double cream	*$\frac{5}{8}$ cup heavy cream*
$\frac{1}{4}$ pint (125 ml.) single cream	*$\frac{5}{8}$ cup light cream*
3 tablespoons brandy or whisky	*3 tablespoons brandy or whisky*
1 tablespoon castor sugar	*1 tablespoon superfine sugar*
12 oz. (300 grms.) ginger nut biscuits	*12 oz. ginger nut cookies*
sliced crystallized ginger	*sliced crystallized ginger*

METHOD

Lightly whip the cream together until it holds its shape, then beat in the brandy or whisky and sugar. Put about 1 heaped teaspoon of the cream mixture on each biscuit (cookie) and sandwich them together to make two long rolls on a serving plate. Spread the remaining cream all over the rolls. Chill in the refrigerator for at least 3 hours. Decorate with the crystallized ginger.

Serves 4 to 6.

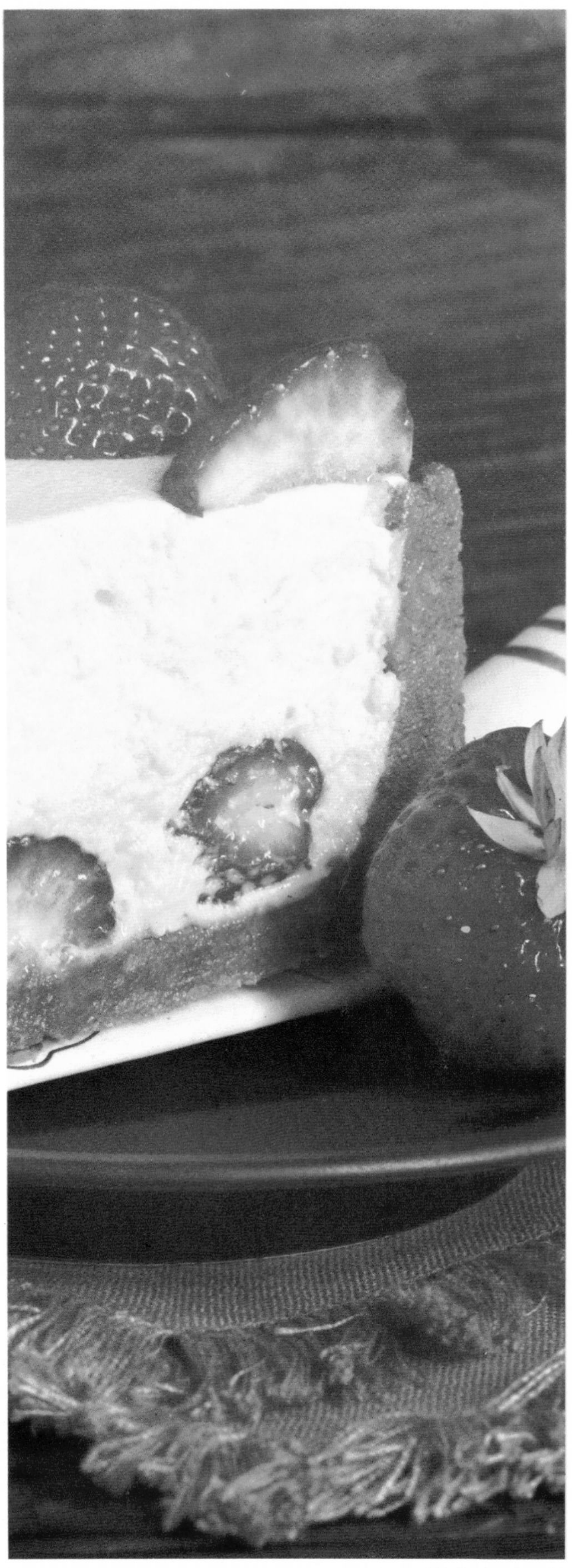

Rich cheesecake

U *is for . . .* UNEXPECTED GUEST:
don't panic – take a look in the storecupboard to see what can be turned into a snack or an impromptu meal

Unexpected Guest

CHILLED 10-MINUTE POTATO SOUP

IMPERIAL/METRIC	AMERICAN
2 tablespoons dehydrated onion	*2 tablespoons dehydrated onion*
1 pint (½ l.) water	*2½ cups water*
1 or 2 chicken stock cubes	*1 or 2 chicken stock cubes*
1 × 5 oz. (125 grms.) packet instant mashed potato	*1 × 5 oz. packet instant mashed potato*
pinch of cayenne pepper	*pinch of cayenne pepper*
¼ pint (125 ml.) single cream	*⅝ cup light cream*
chopped chives or parsley to garnish	*chopped chives or parsley to garnish*

METHOD

Put the onion and water in a saucepan and bring to the boil. Simmer for 5 minutes. Crumble in the stock cubes and add the potato and cayenne pepper. Stir well until all the ingredients are well blended. Chill the soup, then whisk in the cream. Top with the herbs.
Serves 4 to 6.

SALMON CHOWDER

IMPERIAL/METRIC	AMERICAN
1 pint (½ l.) milk	*2½ cups milk*
1 × 11 oz. (275 grms.) can sweetcorn, drained	*1 × 11 oz. can corn, drained*
1 × 7 oz. (175 grms.) can salmon, flaked	*1 × 7 oz. can salmon, flaked*
1 oz. (25 grms.) butter or margarine	*2 tablespoons butter or margarine*
salt and pepper	*salt and pepper*
chopped parsley	*chopped parsley*

METHOD

Put the milk and sweetcorn into a saucepan and bring almost to the boil. Stir in the salmon, butter or margarine, seasoning and parsley. Heat gently for about 5 minutes.
Serves 4.

STORECUPBOARD CASSEROLE

IMPERIAL/METRIC	AMERICAN
½ packet spaghetti sauce mix	*½ packet spaghetti sauce mix*
1 × 14 oz. (350 grms.) can tomatoes	*1 × 14 oz. can tomatoes*
1 × 1 lb. (½ kilo) can cooked ham, diced	*1 × 1 lb. can cooked ham, diced*
1 × 11 oz. (275 grms.) can sweetcorn, drained	*1 × 11 oz. can corn, drained*
½ green pepper, pith and seeds removed and chopped	*½ green pepper, pith and seeds removed and chopped*
1 × 5 oz. (125 grms.) packet instant mashed potato	*1 × 5 oz. packet instant mashed potato*

METHOD

Make up the spaghetti sauce mix with the tomatoes, according to the instructions on the packet. (If you don't have any spaghetti sauce mix, fry a chopped onion in 2 tablespoons of oil until it is soft and translucent, add the tomatoes and a good pinch of mixed herbs and simmer for 15 minutes.) Add the ham with some of the jelly from the can. Don't add too much jelly or the sauce will be too thin. Stir in the corn and pepper. Turn the mixture into an ovenproof dish or casserole. Make up the mashed potato according to the directions on the packet, but add a little milk so that it will be soft enough to spread. Carefully spread the potato over the tomato mixture. Bake in a moderately hot oven, 400°F, Gas Mark 6, for 20 minutes.
Serves 4.

Storecupboard casserole

SPEEDY OMELET

IMPERIAL/METRIC	AMERICAN
3 eggs	*3 eggs*
1 tablespoon water	*1 tablespoon water*
salt and pepper	*salt and pepper*
butter or margarine	*butter or margarine*
Filling	Filling
canned asparagus spears, drained	*canned asparagus spears, drained*
canned potatoes, drained and diced	*canned potatoes, drained and diced*
butter or margarine	*butter or margarine*
2 oz. (50 grms.) Cheddar cheese, diced	*½ cup diced Cheddar cheese*
parsley sprigs	*parsley sprigs*

METHOD

First prepare the filling. Chop the asparagus stalks, reserving the tips for garnish. Fry the diced potatoes in butter or margarine until they are golden. Mix the asparagus, potatoes and cheese together and set aside.

Whisk together the eggs, water and seasoning. Melt butter or margarine in an omelet pan and pour in the egg mixture. When a thin layer has set at the bottom, loosen the mixture from round the edges and tilt the pan so that the liquid egg flows underneath. Spoon the filling on to the omelet while the egg is still soft. Fold and serve garnished with hot asparagus tips and parsley sprigs.

Serves 1 to 2.

Speedy omelet

CORN PAELLA

IMPERIAL/METRIC	AMERICAN
3 to 4 bacon rashers, cut into strips	*3 to 4 bacon slices, cut into strips*
2 oz. (50 grms.) butter or margarine	*¼ cup butter or margarine*
canned potatoes, drained and diced	*canned potatoes, drained and diced*
1 × 11 oz. (275 grms.) can sweetcorn, drained	*1 × 11 oz. can corn, drained*
few olives, sliced	*few olives, sliced*
4 eggs	*4 eggs*
2 oz. (50 grms.) Cheddar cheese, grated	*½ cup grated Cheddar cheese*
salt and pepper	*salt and pepper*

METHOD

Fry the bacon strips in the butter or margarine until they are nearly crisp. Add the potatoes, sweetcorn and olives. Beat the eggs and mix in the cheese and seasoning. Pour the egg mixture over the sweetcorn mixture and cook until it has set.

Serves 4.

Sauces for ice cream

CARAMELLED RICE

IMPERIAL/METRIC	AMERICAN
1 × 15 oz. (375 grms.) can creamed rice or rice pudding	*1 × 15 oz. can creamed rice or rice pudding*
¼ pint (125 ml.) double cream, whipped	*⅝ cup heavy cream, whipped*
3 tablespoons brown sugar	*3 tablespoons brown sugar*
2 tablespoons blanched flaked almonds	*2 tablespoons blanched flaked almonds*

METHOD

Mix together the rice and cream and turn into a shallow flameproof dish. Top with the sugar and nuts and heat gently under the grill (broiler) until golden brown. Serve cold.

Serves 4 to 5.

SAUCES FOR ICE CREAM

Peppermint Sauce

Melt plain or chocolate-coated peppermint creams in a double boiler or basin over hot water. Thin with a little milk or cream.

Jam Sauce

Heat jam with a little fresh lemon or orange juice. Add chopped glacé cherries or nuts.

V *is for* . . . VERY SPECIAL OCCASIONS:
for a celebration such as an anniversary or birthday, don't worry about the expense and make a special effort

Very Special Occasions

Coeur a la creme

COEUR A LA CREME

IMPERIAL/METRIC	AMERICAN
4 oz. (100 grms.) cream cheese	*4 oz. cream cheese*
4 oz. (100 grms.) cottage cheese	*4 oz. cottage cheese*
castor or icing sugar	*superfine or confectioners' sugar*
$\frac{1}{4}$ pint (125 ml.) double cream, whipped	*$\frac{5}{8}$ cup heavy cream, whipped*
8 oz. (200 grms.) strawberries, raspberries or redcurrants	*8 oz. strawberries, raspberries or redcurrants*
sliced Chinese gooseberries	*sliced Chinese gooseberries*
passionfruit	*passionfruit*

METHOD

Rub the cheeses through a sieve and add sugar to taste. Beat in the whipped cream. Divide the mixture between four muslin or cheesecloth lined coeur à la crème moulds (heart-shaped dishes with tiny holes in the bottom). Stand the moulds on a deep plate and place in the refrigerator. Leave to drain for about 12 hours. Turn the cheese hearts out on to serving dishes, peel off the muslin or cheesecloth and garnish with the fruit. Serve with single (light) cream.
Serves 4.

MELON WITH SMOKED HAM

IMPERIAL/METRIC	AMERICAN
1 honeydew or cantaloup melon	*1 honeydew or cantaloup melon*
4 oz. (100 grms.) thinly sliced raw smoked ham, such as Italian proscuitto	*4 oz. thinly sliced raw smoked ham, such as Italian proscuitto*
freshly ground black pepper	*freshly ground black pepper*
black olives	*black olives*

METHOD

Cut the melon into six equal segments and remove the seeds. Chill well. To serve, arrange rolled slices of ham on the melon segments, sprinkle with pepper and garnish with the olives.
Serves 6.

Melon with smoked ham

Lamb in pastry

LAMB IN PASTRY

IMPERIAL/METRIC	AMERICAN
4 lb. (2 kilo) leg of lamb	*4 lb. leg of lamb*
2 oz. (50 grms.) butter or margarine	*$\frac{1}{4}$ cup butter or margarine*
salt and pepper	*salt and pepper*
Pastry	Pastry
10 oz. (250 grms.) flour	*$2\frac{1}{2}$ cups flour*
pinch of salt	*pinch of salt*
2 oz. (50 grms.) butter or margarine	*$\frac{1}{4}$ cup butter or margarine*
3 oz. (75 grms.) lard	*$\frac{3}{8}$ cup shortening*
water	*water*
1 egg, beaten with 1 teaspoon water	*1 egg, beaten with 1 teaspoon water*

METHOD

Have the bone of the leg of lamb cut short and trim off any excess fat. Rub the leg with the butter or margarine and sprinkle with salt and pepper. Place it in a roasting tin and roast in a hot oven, 425°F, Gas Mark 7, for $1\frac{1}{4}$ hours. Cool.

To make the pastry, sift the flour and salt into a bowl. Add the butter or margarine and lard (shortening) and rub in until the mixture resembles fine breadcrumbs. Add enough water to make a firm dough. Roll out the dough into a rectangle large enough to enclose the leg of lamb. Wrap the leg in the dough and place it in the roasting tin with the join underneath. Use the dough trimmings to make a decoration for the top. Prick the dough all over with a knife. Brush with the egg and water mixture and bake in a fairly hot oven, 375°F, Gas Mark 5, for a further 45 minutes.

Serves 8.

BEEF STROGANOFF

IMPERIAL/METRIC	AMERICAN
1 onion, finely chopped	*1 onion, finely chopped*
2 oz. (50 grms.) butter or margarine	*$\frac{1}{4}$ cup butter or margarine*
2 lb. (1 kilo) rump or fillet steak, cut into strips	*2 lb. rump or fillet steak, cut into strips*
4 oz. (100 grms.) mushrooms, sliced	*1 cup sliced mushrooms*
salt and pepper	*salt and pepper*
pinch of grated nutmeg	*pinch of grated nutmeg*
$\frac{1}{2}$ teaspoon dried basil	*$\frac{1}{2}$ teaspoon dried basil*
4 tablespoons beef stock	*4 tablespoons beef stock*
$\frac{1}{2}$ pint (250 ml.) soured cream	*$1\frac{1}{4}$ cups sour cream*
chopped parsley to garnish	*chopped parsley to garnish*

METHOD

Fry the onion in the butter or margarine until soft and translucent. Add the meat and brown quickly, stirring frequently. Add the mushrooms, seasoning, nutmeg, basil and beef stock and stir well. Bring the liquid in the pan to a simmer, then stir in the soured cream. Heat gently but do not allow to boil. Garnish with the parsley.

Serves 4.

Beef stroganoff

Carpetbag steak

CARPETBAG STEAK

IMPERIAL/METRIC	AMERICAN
2 lb. (1 kilo) lean rump or fillet steak, cut about 3 inches ($7\frac{1}{2}$ cm.) thick	*2 lb. lean rump or fillet steak, cut about 3 inches thick*
salt and pepper	*salt and pepper*
12 large oysters	*12 large oysters*
butter or margarine	*butter or margarine*

METHOD

Cut the steak into four pieces. Make a pocket in each piece with a sharp pointed knife. Season the pockets and stuff three oysters into each. Close the pockets with small skewers or wooden toothpicks. Fry the steaks in butter or margarine in a heavy-based frying-pan. Serve topped with extra butter or margarine.
Serves 4.

PROFITEROLES

IMPERIAL/METRIC	AMERICAN
Choux pastry	Choux pastry
2 oz. (50 grms.) butter or margarine	*¼ cup butter or margarine*
¼ pint (125 ml.) mixed milk and water	*⅝ cup mixed milk and water*
2½ oz. (63 grms.) flour, sifted	*½ cup plus 2 tablespoons flour, sifted*
2 eggs, beaten	*2 eggs, beaten*
Filling and icing	Filling and icing
8 oz. (200 grms.) icing sugar	*1½ cups confectioners' sugar*
1 tablespoon cocoa	*1 tablespoon cocoa*
1 tablespoon rum	*1 tablespoon rum*
1 to 2 tablespoons warm water	*1 to 2 tablespoons warm water*
½ pint (250 ml.) double cream, whipped	*1¼ cups heavy cream, whipped*

METHOD

Put the butter or margarine and milk and water mixture in a saucepan and bring to the boil. Remove the pan from the heat and add the flour all at once. Beat the mixture until it forms a ball. Gradually beat in the eggs to make a smooth, shiny paste. Put this dough into a large piping bag with a ½ inch (1¼ cm.) plain nozzle, and pipe 20 blobs on to a greased baking sheet. Alternatively, spoon 20 blobs on to the baking sheet. Bake in a hot oven, 425°F, Gas Mark 7, for 10 minutes, then reduce the oven temperature to fairly hot, 375°F, Gas Mark 5, and bake for a further 15 to 20 minutes or until the puffs are golden brown. Slit one side of each puff so the steam can escape and cool on a wire rack.

To make the icing, sift the icing (confectioners') sugar and cocoa into a bowl. Stir in the rum and enough warm water to make a thick but pourable icing. Fill each puff with whipped cream and pile them up in a pyramid. Dribble over the icing.

Serves 6.

Profiteroles

MELON AMBROSIA

IMPERIAL/METRIC	AMERICAN
1 small rock or cantaloup melon	*1 small rock or cantaloup melon*
1 small honeydew melon	*1 small honeydew melon*
¼ pawpaw or 2 peaches	*¼ pawpaw or 2 peaches*
2 oranges, peeled and segmented	*2 oranges, peeled and segmented*
2 bananas, sliced	*2 bananas, sliced*
6 oz. (150 grms.) strawberries	*6 oz. strawberries*
bunch of black or purple grapes	*bunch of black or purple grapes*
4 tablespoons sugar	*4 tablespoons sugar*
juice of 1 lemon	*juice of 1 lemon*
4 tablespoons desiccated coconut	*4 tablespoons shredded coconut*

METHOD

Remove the skin and seeds from the melons and pawpaw (if using) and cut the flesh into balls or chunks. If using peaches, remove the skin and stones and slice them. Mix all the fruit together, sprinkle with the sugar and lemon juice and toss well. Top with the coconut.

Serves 8 to10.

CHAMPAGNE AND ORANGE JUICE

Mix equal quantities of chilled fresh orange juice and iced Champagne and serve immediately.

W *is for* . . . WEIGHT-WATCHING: *you don't have to limit yourself to cottage cheese, lettuce leaves and crispbread when you're trying to slim* . . . WINE: *the flavour and bouquet of wine can literally transform an ordinary dish*

Watching Your Weight

Eggs with spinach

EGGS WITH SPINACH

IMPERIAL/METRIC	AMERICAN
2 lb. (1 kilo) spinach	*2 lb. spinach*
salt and pepper	*salt and pepper*
$\frac{1}{4}$ *teaspoon grated nutmeg*	$\frac{1}{4}$ *teaspoon grated nutmeg*
1 oz. (25 grms.) margarine	*2 tablespoons margarine*
2 oz. (50 grms.) Parmesan cheese, grated	$\frac{1}{2}$ *cup grated Parmesan cheese*
4 eggs	*4 eggs*

METHOD

Wash the spinach well and put it into a saucepan. (There should be enough water left on the leaves so that you don't need to add any.) Cook for about 10 minutes or until the spinach is tender. Drain thoroughly and chop. Mix the spinach with the seasoning, nutmeg, margarine and almost all the cheese. Divide the spinach mixture between four individual greased ovenproof dishes and make a well in the centres. Break an egg into each and sprinkle with the remaining cheese. Bake in a moderate oven, 350°F, Gas Mark 4, for about 10 minutes or until the eggs are just set.

Serves 4.

CREAMED FISH SOUP

IMPERIAL/METRIC	AMERICAN
8 oz. (200 grms.) white fish fillets, skinned	*8 oz. white fish fillets, skinned*
$1\frac{1}{2}$ *pints* ($\frac{3}{4}$ *l.) fish stock*	*2 pints fish stock*
1 oz. (25 grms.) cornflour	$\frac{1}{4}$ *cup cornstarch*
1 oz. (25 grms.) margarine	*2 tablespoons margarine*
salt and pepper	*salt and pepper*
grated rind of 1 lemon	*grated rind of 1 lemon*
$\frac{1}{2}$ *pint (250 ml.) plain yogurt*	$1\frac{1}{4}$ *cups plain yogurt*
chopped parsley to garnish	*chopped parsley to garnish*

METHOD

Put the fish into a saucepan with about one-third of the fish stock. Bring to the boil and simmer gently until the fish is cooked and flakes easily. Remove the fish from the saucepan, leaving the stock behind. Blend the cornflour (cornstarch) with the remaining fish stock and stir into the stock in the saucepan with the margarine, seasoning and lemon rind. Bring to the boil and simmer, stirring, until slightly thickened. Add the flaked fish and yogurt and stir well. Heat gently but do not allow to boil. Garnish with parsley.

Serves 4.

STUFFED CABBAGE LEAVES

IMPERIAL/METRIC	AMERICAN
4 large cabbage leaves	*4 large cabbage leaves*
2 onions, finely chopped	*2 onions, finely chopped*
2 oz. (50 grms.) margarine	*¼ cup margarine*
8 oz. (200 grms.) lamb's liver, chopped	*8 oz. lamb's liver, chopped*
1 tablespoon tomato paste	*1 tablespoon tomato paste*
1 tablespoon water	*1 tablespoon water*
pinch of grated nutmeg	*pinch of grated nutmeg*
salt and pepper	*salt and pepper*

METHOD

Cook the cabbage leaves in boiling salted water for 5 minutes. Drain and cool, then remove the hard stem from the base of each leaf.

Fry the onions in the margarine until soft and translucent. Add the lamb's liver and fry gently for about 3 minutes, stirring. Stir in the tomato paste, water, nutmeg and seasoning. Cool slightly. Divide the filling between the cabbage leaves. Fold the sides over and roll up. Place the stuffed cabbage leaves in a greased ovenproof dish and bake in a moderate oven, 350°F, Gas Mark 4, for 45 minutes.

Serves 4.

CARROTS VICHY

IMPERIAL/METRIC	AMERICAN
2 oz. (50 grms.) margarine	*¼ cup margarine*
4 tablespoons water	*4 tablespoons water*
1 lb. (½ kilo) carrots, peeled and thinly sliced	*1 lb. carrots, peeled and thinly sliced*
1 artificial sweetener tablet	*1 artificial sweetener tablet*
1 teaspoon salt	*1 teaspoon salt*
¼ teaspoon pepper	*¼ teaspoon pepper*

METHOD

Melt the margarine in a saucepan. Add all the remaining ingredients and mix together. Bring to the boil, then simmer, covered, for 20 minutes or until the carrots are tender.

Serves 4.

MELON AND GRAPES

IMPERIAL/METRIC	AMERICAN
1 honeydew or cantaloup melon	*1 honeydew or cantaloup melon*
1 bunch seedless green grapes, washed and slightly crushed	*1 bunch seedless green grapes, washed and slightly crushed*
1 lemon	*1 lemon*

METHOD

Remove the skin and seeds carefully from the melon and cut the melon flesh into cubes. Mix the melon cubes with the grapes and spoon into four glass serving dishes. Squeeze over lemon juice and chill.

Serves 4.

Stuffed cabbage leaves

Wine for a Change

Coq au vin

COQ AU VIN

IMPERIAL/METRIC	AMERICAN
3 to 4 lb. ($1\frac{1}{2}$ to 2 kilos) roasting chicken	*3 to 4 lb. roasting chicken*
2 oz. (50 grms.) butter or margarine	*$\frac{1}{4}$ cup butter or margarine*
2 tablespoons olive oil	*2 tablespoons olive oil*
4 bacon rashers, cut into strips	*4 bacon slices, cut into strips*
8 pickling onions	*8 baby onions*
2 tablespoons Cognac or brandy	*2 tablespoons Cognac or brandy*
$\frac{3}{4}$ pint (375 ml.) Burgundy	*2 cups Burgundy*
$\frac{1}{4}$ pint (125 ml.) chicken stock	*$\frac{5}{8}$ cup chicken stock*
2 garlic cloves, crushed	*2 garlic cloves, crushed*
bouquet garni	*bouquet garni*
salt and pepper	*salt and pepper*
$1\frac{1}{2}$ tablespoons flour	*$1\frac{1}{2}$ tablespoons flour*
chopped parsley for garnish	*chopped parsley for garnish*

METHOD

Cut the chicken into six pieces. Melt half the butter or margarine with the oil in a flameproof casserole and slowly brown the chicken pieces. Remove them from the casserole and add the bacon strips and onions. Cook, stirring frequently, until they are browned. Return the chicken to the casserole and add the Cognac or brandy. Set it alight, keeping the lid close by in case the flame leaps up. When the flames die down, add the wine, stock, garlic, bouquet garni and seasoning. Cover the casserole and simmer gently for 1 hour or until the chicken pieces are tender.

Blend the remaining butter with the flour to make a smooth paste. Mix this paste with some of the liquid from the casserole, then stir the dissolved paste into the casserole. Simmer, stirring, until the liquid has thickened. Garnish with parsley.

Serves 4 to 6.

MOULES MARINIERES

IMPERIAL/METRIC	AMERICAN
4 dozen mussels	*4 dozen mussels*
$\frac{1}{4}$ pint (125 ml.) white wine	*$\frac{5}{8}$ cup white wine*
$\frac{1}{2}$ pint (250 ml.) water	*$1\frac{1}{4}$ cups water*
bouquet garni	*bouquet garni*
1 carrot, thinly sliced	*1 carrot, thinly sliced*
2 shallots, chopped	*2 shallots, chopped*
1 garlic clove, crushed	*1 garlic clove, crushed*
6 black peppercorns	*6 black peppercorns*
salt	*salt*
3 tablespoons single cream	*3 tablespoons light cream*
1 tablespoon chopped parsley	*1 tablespoon chopped parsley*

METHOD

Scrub the mussels well, removing the beards with a knife as well as any marine growth such as barnacles adhering to the shells. Discard any mussels that have holes in them or are open. Wash the remainder in plenty of cold water. Place the mussels in a wide pan with the wine, water, bouquet garni, carrots, shallots, garlic and peppercorns. Bring to the boil slowly and simmer for 5 minutes, shaking the pan gently until all the shells have opened. Transfer the mussels to a hot serving dish and keep warm. Strain the cooking liquid and return it to the pan. Bring to the boil and boil rapidly until the liquid has reduced by about a third. Stir in salt to taste, the cream and parsley. Pour the sauce over the mussels.

Serves 4.

Moules marinieres

VEAL KIDNEY WITH MARSALA

IMPERIAL/METRIC	AMERICAN
1 lb. (½ kilo) veal kidney	*1 lb. veal kidney*
flour for coating	*flour for coating*
salt and pepper	*salt and pepper*
1 onion, finely chopped	*1 onion, finely chopped*
1 garlic clove, crushed	*1 garlic clove, crushed*
1 oz. (25 grms.) butter or margarine	*2 tablespoons butter or margarine*
4 oz. (100 grms.) button mushrooms, sliced	*1 cup sliced button mushrooms*
4 oz. (100 grms.) bacon, cut into pieces	*4 oz. bacon, cut into pieces*
6 tablespoons Marsala	*6 tablespoons Marsala*
1 tablespoon brandy	*1 tablespoon brandy*

METHOD

Remove the fat and skin from the kidney and cut out the hard core. Coat well with seasoned flour. Fry the onion and garlic in the butter or margarine until soft and translucent. Add the kidney and brown on both sides. Add the mushrooms and bacon pieces and cook, stirring frequently, for 3 minutes. Stir in the Marsala, bring to the boil and simmer very gently for 25 to 30 minutes or until the kidney is tender. Stir in the brandy and correct the seasoning.

Serves 4.

PEACHES IN WINE

IMPERIAL/METRIC	AMERICAN
4 large, ripe peaches	*4 large, ripe peaches*
castor sugar	*superfine sugar*
lemon juice	*lemon juice*
red or rosé wine or chilled white dessert wine	*red or rosé wine or chilled white dessert wine*

METHOD

Peel the peaches carefully and slice them into four glass serving dishes or goblets. Sprinkle with sugar and lemon juice. Just before serving, pour enough wine into the dishes or goblets to reach the top of the fruit.

Serves 4.

Veal kidney with marsala

XYZ is for . . . YESTERDAY'S LEFTOVERS: *don't throw away the leftover roast meat or cooked vegetables – turn them into something adventurous and different*

Yesterday's Leftovers

Nasi goreng

NASI GORENG

IMPERIAL/METRIC

8 oz. (200 grms.) onions, finely chopped
4 oz. (100 grms.) butter or margarine
8 oz. (200 grms.) cooked pork or ham, diced
2 to 3 tablespoons curry powder
pinch of cayenne pepper
pinch of chilli powder
2 tablespoons Worcestershire or soya sauce
few drops Tabasco sauce
salt
12 oz. (300 grms.) cooked rice
12 oz. (300 grms.) mixed cooked vegetables
3 tomatoes, quartered
strips of pancake (optional)

AMERICAN

8 oz. onions, finely chopped
½ cup butter or margarine
1 cup diced cooked pork or ham
2 to 3 tablespoons curry powder
pinch of cayenne pepper
pinch of chilli powder
2 tablespoons Worcestershire or soy sauce
few drops Tabasco sauce
salt
4 cups cooked rice
3 cups mixed cooked vegetables
3 tomatoes, quartered
strips of crêpe (optional)

METHOD

Fry the onions in half of the butter or margarine until soft and translucent. Add the pork or ham, curry powder, cayenne pepper, chilli powder, Worcestershire or soya sauce, Tabasco sauce and salt and cook over low heat, stirring frequently, for 5 minutes. Stir in the remaining butter or margarine, the rice and vegetables and cook, stirring, until the mixture is hot and well blended. Spoon into a hot serving dish and place the tomato wedges around the edge. If you like, arrange strips of pancake (crêpe) across the top in a criss-cross fashion.

Serves 5 to 6.

GOOSE OR TURKEY PATE

IMPERIAL/METRIC

4 oz. (100 grms.) butter or margarine
8oz. (200 grms.) cooked goose or turkey, minced or finely chopped
1 tablespoon dry sherry
pinch of ground cloves
pinch of black pepper
½ teaspoon salt
½ teaspoon lemon juice
2 drops Tabasco sauce
2 oz. (50 grms.) melted butter or margarine

AMERICAN

½ cup butter or margarine
8 oz. cooked goose or turkey, ground or finely chopped
1 tablespoon dry sherry
pinch of ground cloves
pinch of black pepper
½ teaspoon salt
½ teaspoon lemon juice
2 drops Tabasco sauce
¼ cup melted butter or margarine

METHOD

Cream the butter or margarine well and beat in the goose or turkey, sherry, cloves, pepper, salt, lemon juice and Tabasco sauce. Divide the mixture between four individual pots and smooth the tops. Pour over the melted butter or margarine. Cover with clear plastic wrap or aluminium foil and chill in the refrigerator. Serve with crisp hot toast.

Serves 4.

MOUSSAKA

IMPERIAL/METRIC	AMERICAN
1 lb. ($\frac{1}{2}$ kilo) aubergines, thinly sliced	*1 lb. eggplants, thinly sliced*
oil for frying	*oil for frying*
2 large onions, thinly sliced	*2 large onions, thinly sliced*
1 garlic clove, crushed	*1 garlic clove, crushed*
1 lb. ($\frac{1}{2}$ kilo) minced cooked lamb	*1 lb. ground cooked lamb*
1 × 14 oz. (350 grms.) can tomatoes	*1 × 14 oz. can tomatoes*
2 tablespoons tomato purée	*2 tablespoons tomato purée*
dash of Tabasco sauce	*dash of Tabasco sauce*
salt and pepper	*salt and pepper*
2 eggs	*2 eggs*
$\frac{1}{4}$ pint (125 ml.) single cream	*$\frac{5}{8}$ cup light cream*
2 oz. (50 grms.) Cheddar cheese, grated	*$\frac{1}{2}$ cup grated Cheddar cheese*
3 tablespoons Parmesan cheese, grated	*3 tablespoons grated Parmesan cheese*

METHOD

Fry one-third of the aubergines (eggplants) in oil for 3 to 4 minutes, turning once, until they are lightly browned. Remove from the pan and drain well. Fry and drain the remaining aubergines (eggplants) in the same way. Fry the onions and garlic in 1 tablespoon oil until pale golden brown. Stir in the lamb, tomatoes, tomato purée and Tabasco sauce. Bring to the boil and simmer, uncovered, for 20 minutes. Season well.

Arrange alternate layers of aubergines (eggplants) and the lamb mixture in an ovenproof dish. Beat the eggs and cream together and stir in the cheese. Pour this mixture on to the moussaka. Bake in a moderate oven, 350°F, Gas Mark 4, for 35 to 40 minutes, or until the topping is well risen and golden brown.
Serves 4.

Meat balls with spaghetti

MEAT BALLS WITH SPAGHETTI

IMPERIAL/METRIC	AMERICAN
1 lb, ($\frac{1}{2}$ kilo) cooked beef, veal or pork	*1 lb. cooked beef, veal or pork*
1 to 2 garlic cloves	*1 to 2 garlic cloves*
2 to 3 parsley sprigs	*2 to 3 parsley sprigs*
thin slice lemon rind	*thin slice lemon rind*
1 apple, peeled and cored	*1 apple, peeled and cored*
1 large slice white bread, soaked in a little milk	*1 large slice white bread, soaked in a little milk*
1 egg, lightly beaten	*1 egg, lightly beaten*
salt and pepper	*salt and pepper*
pinch of grated nutmeg	*pinch of grated nutmeg*
flour for coating	*flour for coating*
oil for frying	*oil for frying*
12 oz. (300 grms.) spaghetti	*12 oz. spaghetti*
butter or margarine	*butter or margarine*
chopped parsley to garnish	*chopped parsley to garnish*
Tomato sauce	Tomato sauce
2 lb. (1 kilo) ripe tomatoes, chopped	*2 lb. ripe tomatoes, chopped*
1 small onion, finely chopped	*1 small onion, finely chopped*
1 carrot, peeled and chopped	*1 carrot, peeled and chopped*
1 celery stalk, chopped	*1 celery stalk, chopped*
$\frac{1}{2}$ teaspoon dried basil	*$\frac{1}{2}$ teaspoon dried basil*
pinch of sugar	*pinch of sugar*
salt and pepper	*salt and pepper*

METHOD

First make the tomato sauce. Put all the ingredients into a saucepan and bring to the boil. Simmer until the mixture is almost a purée, then pass it through a sieve and correct the seasoning.

Put the meat, garlic, parsley, lemon rind and apple through a fine mincer or food mill. Squeeze any excess milk from the bread and add it to the meat mixture with the egg, seasoning and nutmeg. Mix well together with your hands, then form the mixture into balls. Roll the balls in flour, then fry them until they are well browned. Drain the meat balls on absorbent paper, then add them to the tomato sauce. Simmer very gently for 10 to 15 minutes.

Meanwhile, cook the spaghetti in plenty of boiling salted water for 8 to 12 minutes, or until it is tender but still firm. Drain thoroughly and transfer to a hot serving dish. Add a generous lump of butter or margarine and toss well. Arrange the meat balls on top of the spaghetti, pour over the tomato sauce and sprinkle with the parsley.
Serves 4.

CREAM OF CHICKEN SOUP

IMPERIAL/METRIC

carcass of a cooked chicken with giblets (if available)
about 3 pints (¾ l.) water
salt and pepper
1 to 2 onions, halved
1 to 2 carrots
bouquet garni
1 oz. (25 grms.) flour
½ pint (250 ml.) single or double cream
2 egg yolks

AMERICAN

carcass of a cooked chicken with giblets (if available)
about 3¾ pints water
salt and pepper
1 to 2 onions, halved
1 to 2 carrots
bouquet garni
¼ cup flour
1¼ cups light or heavy cream
2 egg yolks

METHOD

Put the carcass and giblets in a large saucepan and cover with the water. Add the seasoning, onions, carrots and bouquet garni. Bring to the boil, cover and simmer for at least 2 hours. Strain and discard the flavourings and carcass. Any chicken meat may be chopped and added to the stock. Mix the flour with a little of the stock and add to the remaining stock. Cook, stirring, until slightly thickened, then remove the pan from the heat. Blend the cream and egg yolks together and whisk into the soup.
Serves 6.

Courgettes (Zucchini) with ham

COURGETTES (ZUCCHINI) WITH HAM

IMPERIAL/METRIC

1 lb. ($\frac{1}{2}$ kilo) courgettes, sliced
flour for coating
salt and pepper
2 onions, finely chopped
1 garlic clove, crushed
oil for frying
8 oz. (200 grms.) cooked ham, cut into pieces
2 oz. (50 grms.) Parmesan cheese, grated

AMERICAN

1 lb. zucchini, sliced
flour for coating
salt and pepper
2 onions, finely chopped
1 garlic clove, crushed
oil for frying
8 oz. cooked ham, cut into pieces
$\frac{1}{2}$ cup grated Parmesan cheese

METHOD

Coat the courgette (zucchini) slices with seasoned flour. Fry the onions and garlic in a little oil until soft and translucent. Add the pieces of ham and brown lightly. Transfer the ham and onions to a plate. Add a little more oil to the pan and lightly brown the courgette (zucchini) slices. Arrange most of the courgette (zucchini) slices in a buttered ovenproof dish. Sprinkle with half the onion and half the Parmesan cheese. Put the ham on top, then the remaining onion and cheese, and finally the rest of the courgette (zucchini) slices. Bake in a moderate oven, 350°F, Gas Mark 4, for 15 minutes.

Serves 4.

Savoury pancake boat

SAVOURY PANCAKE BOAT

IMPERIAL/METRIC	AMERICAN
Batter	Batter
4 oz. (100 grms.) flour	*1 cup flour*
pinch of salt	*pinch of salt*
1 egg	*1 egg*
½ pint (250 ml.) milk, or milk and water mixed	*1¼ cups milk, or milk and water mixed*
1 oz. (25 grms.) cooking fat	*2 tablespoons cooking fat*
Filling	Filling
3 oz. (75 grms.) butter or margarine	*⅜ cup butter or margarine*
2 oz. (50 grms.) flour	*½ cup flour*
½ pint (250 ml.) chicken stock	*1¼ cups chicken stock*
¼ pint (125 ml.) milk	*⅝ cup milk*
4 to 6 oz. (100 to 150 grms.) cooked chicken or fish, diced	*½ to ¾ cup diced cooked chicken or fish*
2 to 3 tablespoons single cream	*2 to 3 tablespoons light cream*
salt and pepper	*salt and pepper*
4 oz. (100 grms.) button mushrooms, sliced	*1 cup sliced button mushrooms*
4 hard-boiled eggs, cut into wedges	*4 hard-boiled eggs, cut into wedges*
chopped parsley and sprigs of watercress to garnish	*chopped parsley and sprigs of watercress to garnish*

METHOD

To make the batter, sift the flour and salt into a mixing bowl. Make a well in the centre and add the egg and some of the liquid. Mix together, gradually incorporating the flour. Add the remaining liquid and beat thoroughly to a smooth batter. Melt the cooking fat in a shallow baking tin and pour the batter into it. Bake towards the top of a hot to very hot oven, 450 to 475°F, Gas Mark 7 to 8, for 15 minutes. Then reduce the heat to moderate, 350°F, Gas Mark 4, and bake for a further 10 to 15 minutes, or until the pancake boat is well risen and browned.

Meanwhile, make the filling. Melt two-thirds of the butter or margarine and stir in the flour. Cook gently, stirring, for 1 minute. Gradually stir in the chicken stock and milk and bring to the boil. Simmer, stirring constantly, until the sauce is thickened and smooth. Stir in the chicken or fish, cream and seasoning. Heat gently but do not allow to boil.

Fry the mushrooms in the remaining butter or margarine and add to the chicken or fish mixture with most of the egg wedges. Mix well. Transfer the baked pancake boat to a hot serving dish and spoon the filling over it. Top with the remaining egg wedges and garnish with the parsley and watercress.

Serves 6.

Index

First published by Octopus Books Limited
This edition published by Cathay Books
59 Grosvenor Street, London W1.

Reprinted 1981
ISBN 0 904644 03 0

Printed in Hong Kong

Acknowledgements

Angel Studio: 46–7, 83
Argentine Beef Bureau: 69
Birds Eye: 13
Cadbury Schweppes Food Advisory Service: 84, 115
Copha of E.O.I. Pty. Ltd.: 28–9
Dutch Dairy Bureau: 43, 122
Electricity Council's photographic unit (Jerry Tan): 53
Flour Advisory Bureau: 73
Fruit Producers' Council: 4, 123
Lawry's Foods Inc.: 17, 48, 107, 113
Lea & Perrins Worcestershire Sauce: 45
National Dairy Council: 34
New Zealand Lamb Information Bureau: 112
Paf International: 40, 54, 97, 116, 120–1, 124–5
RHM Foods Ltd: 9, 16
Syndication International: 7, 24, 26, 29, 57, 87, 105, 119, 126
Tabasco Pepper Sauce: 25
T. Wall & Son (Meat & Handy Food) Ltd: 104
John West Foods Ltd: 50, 68–9, 108

PDO 81-823